KETO
FAT BOMBS,
SWEETS & TREATS

KETO
FAT BOMBS,
SWEETS & TREATS

**OVER 100 RECIPES AND IDEAS FOR LOW-CARB
BREADS, CAKES, COOKIES, AND MORE**

URVASHI PITRE

Photography by Ghazalle Badiozamani

HOUGHTON MIFFLIN HARCOURT
BOSTON   NEW YORK   2019

Copyright © 2019 by Urvashi Pitre

Photography © 2019 by Ghazalle Badiozamani

Food styling by Monica Pierini

Prop styling by Jenna Tedesco

For information about permission to reproduce selections from this book, write to trade.permissions@hmhco.com or to Permissions, Houghton Mifflin Harcourt Publishing Company, 3 Park Avenue, 19th Floor, New York, New York 10016.

hmhbooks.com

Library of Congress Cataloging-in-Publication Data is available.

ISBN 978-0-358-07430-4 (pbk)

ISBN 978-0-358-07433-5 (ebk)

Book design by Jennifer K. Beal Davis

Printed in The United States of America

DOC 10 9 8 7 6 5 4 3 2 1

4500749501

To my mother, Veena Pitre. Even though I complained,
I'm really glad you "voluntold" me to cook nightly.

CONTENTS

CAKES, COOKIES & BROWNIES 90

CHOCOLATES & FAT BOMBS 132

DRINKS, ICE CREAM & ICE POPS 156

FROSTINGS & GLAZES 186

PUDDINGS & PIES 202

KETO SHAKES & SMOOTHIES 240

KETO SALAD DRESSINGS 244

INDEX 250

ACKNOWLEDGMENTS

There are so many people to thank for this book.

As always, I thank the Universe for the constant, unwavering support of my husband Roger, and my son Alex.

Thanks to John Kasinger and Lisa Kinglsley for helping me test and finesse the recipes.

My agent, Stacey Glick, thank you so much for your continuing support.

My editor, Justin Schwartz, with whom I hope to do more books that are not crashes. To our continued partnership and success!

Ghazalle Badiozamani and her team of accomplished stylists and helpers make my food look pretty—not just tasty. Thank you to Monica Pieroni, Leila Clifford, Jenna Tedesco, and Bridget Kenny for your great work.

Thanks also to the whole army at Houghton Mifflin Harcourt, which helped without my even realizing it, to make this book a reality.

And of course, to my fans, followers, and readers who continue to support, suggest, encourage, and make me laugh daily.

INTRODUCTION

You can be an accomplished career woman, a great mother, and the best friend ever. You can speak six languages and dance backward in high heels. But if you're overweight, chances are, that's the first thing people notice about you. For many people, that's the last thing they'll notice about you as well. It's so easy to be dismissed as "less than" when you're carrying extra weight. I think this is due to the prevalent belief in our society that people are overweight because they lack self-control or discipline.

I assure you, I do not lack self-control. I am extremely disciplined. I rose to the top of my career as chief marketing information officer for a large advertising agency by dint of great discipline and a work ethic that had me working 16- to 18-hour days, in addition to trying to be a good mother. But I am quite sure that when I first walked into a room, what people probably noticed about me was the 80 extra pounds I was carrying.

The idea that those who weigh more got that way because they eat more is also well-entrenched in our belief system. So much so that people will discount the evidence before them and continue to believe the myth that overweight = overeater, and that's why they got to be overweight. My colleagues loved going out with me for meals. Many would ask what I planned to have and order something different. They did this because they knew they would finish their food, and then they'd eat half of mine since I never finished my portion. These same people spent days on end with me on business trips, where we all spent hours together and ate together. They saw what I ate. It was less than what most of them ate.

Yet I was overweight, and they were not.

What do you want to bet that some of them thought I secretly ate late at night, in my hotel room? (For the record, I did not.) Be honest, wouldn't you have believed that? I was never someone who ate an entire large pizza by myself. I have never polished off a cake without sharing. I have never even eaten a whole pint of ice cream by myself. I was not a binge eater. I did not eat in secret. I didn't exceed normal portions.

In a society where we firmly believe in the "All calories are equal" and "Expend more calories as you ingest" theories of weight loss, people will discount your behavior, and continue to believe that if you are overweight, you're eating more than those who are not overweight. There are many other explanations for why people become overweight. In my case, the explanations were simple—but it took me years to identify them.

During those years, I followed every eating style dictated by "experts." I tried vegetarian, paleo, starvation, vegan diets. I tried eating five small meals. I ate less than 800 calories a day, and during a few horrible months, I tried eating 2,500 calories a day because I was told I needed to "fuel my metabolism." I tried it all.

But the weight did not come off.

There was one thing I never tried—and that was a ketogenic diet. Part of this was my natural inclination to eat a vegetarian diet over a carnivorous diet. There is nothing wrong with a delicious vegetarian diet—unless, like me, you are extremely carbohydrate sensitive and insulin resistant. Then, eating brown rice and beans is probably not the best for you. It certainly wasn't the best thing for me.

The other part of it was, I didn't believe it would work for me, since I had failed with so many other things. My inability to lose weight—my failure to, as I saw it—weighed on me. I hate failing; I mean, we all do, but I *HATE* failing! I take it very personally and I get obsessed with it, and it's . . . well, let's just say it's not pretty.

In desperation, I decided to have weight loss surgery. I felt I had exhausted every other avenue. But before I did that, I had to understand that the surgery by itself would accomplish little. By dint of enforcing fasting, it might help me in the early days after surgery. But over time, it is entirely possible to put back on the weight if you don't change your eating habits. I heard many stories from people who had put back on all—if not more of—the weight, even after surgery. Every physician I spoke to was quite clear that surgery by itself would not do the trick—I had to embrace a ketogenic diet.

My weight issues were probably linked to my untreated hypothyroidism, my extreme carb-sensitivity, and my insulin resistance. There is one way of eating that is beneficial for all these conditions—and that is a ketogenic diet.

Five years ago, once I accepted that I would have to change my diet forever, my husband and I had vertical sleeve surgery. We embraced a keto/low-carb diet, changed the way we ate all together, and accepted that this was our eating style going forward.

I still struggle with my weight every day. I still have to monitor what I eat, I still have to track, and, when I fall off the wagon, I still gain weight. I can eat very few calories, but if my carbohydrate intake goes up, I gain weight.

In my Facebook groups, I speak openly about the difficulty of staying keto and/or low-carb over a sustained period of time. In my case, "carbohydrate addiction" is not far from the truth. I do crave carbs. (Yes, I do understand it may not be a scientific construct, but behaviorally, for all intents and purposes, I have been known to act as though I am addicted. One cupcake is not enough, and one cupcake is also one too many.)

I have to be ever-vigilant. I have to stay on guard. I have to accept that it will take me a month to lose what I gain in a week of indulgence. It is frustrating, it is unfair—but that is my reality.

Does all this sounds familiar to you? Have you had similar struggles, a similar story, a similar path toward keto? Are you still struggling with the unfairness of it all?

Let's talk about that unfairness.

WEIGHT GAIN AND ANGER

I don't see people speaking about this openly, but I am sure that I am not the only one who has experienced this. When surrounded by thin people who seemingly eat whatever they want and stay skinny, while you watch every calorie that goes into your mouth, it is difficult to not be angry, to not rail at the universe, to not have a little pity party about how unfair things are and how unlucky you are to gain weight so easily.

I will admit that there were times it was difficult for me to even think about what to do to lose weight, because thinking about it would fill me with anger. Why was I so unlucky? Why was my metabolism so efficient that it was apparently able to survive and even thrive on starvation-level calories? This was patently unfair and I just absolutely did not deserve this fate.

I know, I know. We tell our children the world is not fair. You'd think we'd know better. The fact is, our heads might know better, but internalizing that in our hearts is not the same thing.

This continued for years, which is both ridiculous and shameful, really, a grown woman railing against the unfairness in the world for being overweight. Then one day, I realized that if I were going to complain about fairness, perhaps I could also complain about all the unfair *advantages* that have been afforded to me. Clearly I won the "lottery of the womb" when I was born into an educated, intelligent, nurturing, middle-class family. Clearly I had had many lucky breaks come my way, in my personal life, in my career, in my choices of friends, in a thousand different facets of my life. Somehow I never complained about the inherent unfairness of luck—just about the one thing where I had not, in fact, won the genetic lottery! Yeah, way to be overprivileged *and* ignorant about it, Urvashi. This changed my attitude and prepared me mentally to be where

I could put aside the matter of fairness or lack thereof and focus on what I could do, rather than why I should not have to do anything at all in the first place.

I mention all this because in conversations with others I have realized that this is a deterrent for many of us. The sheer unfairness, the refusal to accept that some of us just need to make more radical changes than others in order to lose weight, the belief that we should be able to eat like others and have our bodies deal with foods like others' seem to—all these things keep us from accepting the truth, and moving on to doing what is needed.

If you are struggling with these thought patterns and issues, I recommend that part of your recovery and the foundation for the dietary change you need to make in your life will need to involve acceptance of your metabolism. Without this acceptance, you will be tempted to "eat like other people," to believe you can do what others do, to think it's unfair and therefore that you should not have to change.

Know that you are not alone. For many of us, what is needed is strict control over carbohydrates. Many of us gain weight on not much food, especially if it's the wrong type of food. Many of us absolutely cannot and should not be eating five times a day. Many of us do not lose 50 pounds in three months. Many of us stall for weeks on end, even though we are doing the right things. If you are one of those people, you are one of my tribe. You and I may have to eat differently, eat less often, fast for long periods of time, and monitor our intake carefully—for the rest of our lives.

So let's talk about what needs doing to lose this weight, and/or to keep it off. The first thing that is required is a better understanding of why we gain weight.

UNDERSTANDING THE MECHANICS OF WEIGHT LOSS

I like to understand why things work as they do. Simply giving me rules just doesn't work for me. In fact, I'm so terrible at following rules that telling me the rule is a surefire way to make me tune out or blatantly disobey you. But tell me *why*, and I'm a happy, nerdy scientist at that point. Basically I'll listen to science before I will listen to what your neighbor told you or what you think is true.

So let me tell you what I wish someone had told me about the mechanics of weight loss, if you are overweight due to carbohydrate/insulin disturbances.

Here they are:

1. Your body is either releasing insulin or it is not.
2. If it's releasing insulin, you're not burning fat.
3. If you fast or eat foods that don't cause you to release insulin, you will probably burn fat.

That's all I needed to know, rather than all the "Eat this, don't eat that, eat carbs only during a full moon while facing west" stuff that I was busy memorizing and trying to live by. Everything else about weight loss and the ketogenic diet focuses on the details of how to keep your insulin levels low.

- You restrict carbs because carbs cause you to release insulin.
- You eat moderate amounts of protein because excess protein can cause you to release insulin.
- You eat more fat because fat does not cause you to release insulin.
- You pair the ketogenic diet with intermittent fasting and/or no grazing between meals to reduce insulin secretion and increase insulin sensitivity.

THIS IS THE BIG PICTURE.

KETO
BASICS

The ketogenic (keto) diet is based on a normal metabolic process called *ketosis,* which happens when your body does not have enough glucose for energy and therefore burns fat instead. During ketosis, chemical molecules called *ketones* are produced in the liver when the fat is burned, and they are sent into your bloodstream to be used as fuel for the brain, muscles, and tissues.

Ketosis is probably what allowed our ancestors to survive when carbohydrates were not readily available for long stretches of time. A keto diet reduces carbohydrate intake to encourage the body to burn fat instead.

MACRONUTRIENTS

The keto diet is a low-carb, moderate-protein, high-fat plan, which usually breaks down into the following percentages daily:

- 60 to 75 percent of calories from fat
- 15 to 30 percent of calories from protein
- 5 to 10 percent of calories from carbs

Every single meal does not have to be in perfect balance, but the proportions of macronutrients—carbohydrates, protein, and fat, or your "macros"—should be close to these percentages at the end of the day.

SETTING THE RIGHT MACROS FOR YOU

Everyone has unique keto macronutrient proportions to produce the desired effects (such as weight loss or maintenance), depending on height, weight, goals, exercise level, and body fat percentage. This is why using an online keto calculator can be very effective for figuring out your individual dietary needs. These calculators can calculate your macro numbers and daily calorie count to keep you in the state of ketosis, or get you there initially.

Since carbohydrates (glucose) are the usual primary fuel source for the body, it is important to stay within the recommended macro range when considering your food choices. If your carbs are too high, you will not reach ketosis at all.

Some people go into ketosis with 20 grams of carbs daily, while other lucky folks seem to be able to get there with twice as many carbs. The right level of carbs for ketosis and health definitely seems to fluctuate for people, but with a little experimenting, you will find your own sweet spot for weight loss/maintenance and good health.

After a lot of experimenting, I know what works for me. I started the journey at 5 feet 5 inches tall and 230 pounds. My goal weight was 152 pounds, which I reached over ten interminable, difficult months. To achieve weight loss, I had to eat less than 800 calories per day and keep carbs between 20 and 25 grams. For maintenance, I can eat 1,200 to 1,300 calories per day and keep carbs between 50 and 75 grams. I still gain when I routinely consume 80 grams of carbs or more per day.

To lose a small regain in weight now, I have to fast intermittently every other day and restrict carbs to 20 to 30 grams per day until the gain is gone. Knowing this has helped me maintain my weight over the past five years. Clearly what works for me may not work for you, but if you track your intake carefully, you will soon know what is best for you.

I taught myself how to follow the keto diet by consulting three sources:

- *The Obesity Code* by Jason Fung
- *Why We Get Fat: And What to Do About It* by Gary Taubes
- *The Art and Science of Low Carbohydrate Living* by Jeff S. Volek and Stephen D. Phinney

These sources provide the scientific rationale and research that underlie their recommendations, which I appreciate and you may too.

KETO MYTHS

There are as many myths about keto as there are adherents to the diet. Some may see what I write below as a myth as well, but I want to share my perspective, so you understand how I approached this book and my recipes.

Myth #1: Keto and Low-Carb Are Entirely Different Things.

These diets may be somewhat different, mainly with respect to whether or not they specify a per-day carb cap. The keto diet generally requires you to stay at or below 20 to 50 grams of net carbs per day. Low-carb diets simply exhort you to eat fewer carbs. Often, the standard American diet (SAD) is used as a yardstick. Average consumption of carbohydrates is estimated at 300 grams daily for most Americans. As you can see, there's a lot of room between 20 grams and 300 grams to specify what constitutes low-carb. Keto and nonspecific low-carb diets are similar in that they typically emphasize consuming lower amounts of carbohydrates, similar amounts of proteins, and higher quantities of fat than are consumed in the SAD.

Myth #2: Certain Ingredients Are Simply Not "Allowed" on Keto.

Religion, politics, and keto diet rules—these are the known controversies we all avoid discussing with others, aren't they? Here's my approach to keto: I completely exclude excessively high–glycemic index foods such as pasta, rice, potatoes, bread, flour, and sugar. These foods are known to spike blood sugar and insulin for absolutely everyone. I advocate not eating sugar, not even in small quantities. Sugar causes a spike in insulin and often results in cravings for more sugar that can derail a well-progressing keto dieter.

Other than that, I eat real food, and I watch macros carefully. What matters to me is that the overall carb count remains low, and that what carbs I do ingest are from foods that are not known to spike insulin levels (such as vegetables, berries, etc.).

I also count net carbs, which is total carbs, minus fiber, minus sugar alcohols. If you're on a keto diet for health reasons, you should do what your doctor tells you. Me, I'm the wrong kind of doctor to give you advice on that. (If you have issues with your experimental design or statistical significance, however, I'm your girl.)

Myth #3: Eating Keto Means I Have to Eat All the Fat Grams My Calculator Specifies.

Most experts agree that we should eat only as much fat as is needed for satiety, especially if you are trying to lose weight. Your goal is to get your body to burn stored fat. This is much harder than burning the fat you eat, which is more readily available for fuel. So your highly efficient body is going to burn the fat you eat for fuel before it starts tapping into your stored reserves. If you keep eating more fat than your body needs to burn for fuel, not only will you not lose fat, but you could gain some fat, which is not what you're going for. The main reason fat makes up such a high proportion of keto diets is because it does not raise insulin. If you're hungry, fat not only satiates quickly, but it does so without raising insulin secretion.

What works for me is to treat protein as a level I have to hit, carbs as a level I cannot exceed, and then fat to satiate my hunger— and you know, because it tastes so good!

Myth #4: Calories Don't Matter.

Sadly, calories do still matter, for the most part. The type of calories you eat (those from carbs versus protein versus fat) matters quite a lot. We all know that 100 calories of broccoli has a very different impact on your blood sugar and insulin than 100 calories of sugar.

But having said that, it is simply not possible to lose weight while eating many more calories than your body can burn. Keto allows me to eat more calories and yet not gain weight than I can on a high-carb diet. But if you eat 4,000 calories in a day, and your basal metabolic rate (BMR, or the number of calories needed for your body to perform basic, life-sustaining functions, like

you know, breathing, processing food, etc.) is only 2,000 calories, it's only a matter of time before you will be shopping for new pants.

While it may sound odd that I'm saying this at the beginning of my own dessert book, I want you to use the desserts in this book just as you would have when you weren't doing keto—they're not an every-meal, unlimited occurrence. While all the recipes in this book are high-fat, moderate-protein, and low-carb, many of them are not exactly low-calorie.

What works for me is to use them as a treat or an indulgence, especially when I'm craving something carby. I might allow myself a small fat bomb every day—but cake and cookies are still not an everyday food for me, even on keto.

Myth #5: Higher Levels of Ketosis for the Win!

Higher levels of ketones do not cause greater fat loss. Being in ketosis is much more impor-tant than the level of that ketosis. While it's fun to pee on the keto screening strips and brag about the various colors your strips turn, recognize this for what it is—fun and games. As long as you are in ketosis, you are burning fat.

A 4-WEEK PLAN FOR EASING INTO KETO

When my boys were little, I taught them both to read. Mark was reading by the time he was 2½ years old, and Alex by the time he was 3½ (I wasn't able to stay home with him, so it took us a little longer). I taught them using a series called *Bob Books*. The principle of the books is that they start with two consonants and a vowel, and an entire book is written with just those three sounds. Book 2 adds a few additional sounds, and this continues with additional books until the boys were reading effortlessly.

This build-on-it pedagogical approach made it so easy for the boys to keep reading and to keep learning. I also saw the sense of pride they had in reading a whole book by themselves. It reemphasized for me the need for us all to experience small victories as we build a feeling of self-efficacy while learning a new skill.

Weight loss is a long, drawn-out process. If your only milestone is that you will celebrate when you reach a 50-pound loss, you will be waiting for a long while, and you may get a little discouraged. Instead, I am a firm believer in celebrating NSVs, or non-scale victories.

NSVs include fitting into smaller clothes even though the scale hasn't moved. Going for a long walk, turning down your favorite pasta, feeling better than you have in years, joints that aren't swollen—all these are great and delightful NSVs that you can focus on.

These are important because much of weight loss, especially the *pace* of weight loss, is often something you can't dictate as much as you'd like to.

WHAT YOU CAN AND CAN'T CONTROL

I want you to listen to me carefully on this. You cannot fully control how fast your body wants to lose weight. You can only control what you put in your mouth—or don't put in your mouth.

If you're anything like me and a thousand other slow losers, you could do everything you're meant to—and stall, lose one week but not other weeks, lose slower than other people, and otherwise get utterly discouraged.

Your body has its own rhythm, its own rate of weight loss. You can control what you eat or don't eat. You cannot dictate to your body how fast it should lose weight.

So I have to judge my success not just on the scale, but in behavioral changes. As a cognitive psychologist, I am a huge proponent of behavioral therapy as a way to achieve sustainable behavioral change.

Change your behavior, change your eating habits, change what you eat and when you eat, and health and weight loss will follow.

This chapter focuses on how to make these behavioral changes in a manner that is sustainable, gentle, and effective.

Before you start, I should mention something: I am not a medical or healthcare professional, so you definitely want to consult what my sons call "a real doctor, not a PhD like my mom." My only objective here is to show people how easy it can be to start on keto using baby steps and achievable goals.

EASING INTO KETO

Some of us want to jump straight into keto, while others are better off easing into it slowly. We worry that we will start something we won't be able to keep up with, and we use that as an excuse to never start.

If you are someone who prefers easing into keto, I want to share with you the plan that thousands of people have followed, with great success, within my TwoSleevers Facebook keto group. It is a gentle, but effective way to change around your eating habits. Many have also used it successfully to bring reluctant family members on board.

Each week, I will give you three or four things that you will want to do. By the end of four weeks, you will be eating almost entirely keto, and tracking your macros to ensure that you are on track.

I know these tips look ridiculously simple—but they work. There are volumes written on eat this, not that, do this or that, don't eat this particular food unless it's a full moon—but really, there's no need to complicate things that much.

#trustUrvashi, as we say in my Facebook groups. Follow these tips and you will be on your way to good health.

Week 1 Tips

1. *Don't eat:* This week, don't eat potatoes, pasta, bread, rice, grains, beans, and sugar, and limit fruits to two per day.

2. *Do eat:* Eat whatever you want for meats, eggs, vegetables, cheese, nuts, avocados, and fats. Eat meat, nuts, and cheese for snacks between meals if you get hungry.

3. *Find recipes:* Go to my website TwoSleevers.com and find the 170+ keto, low-carb recipes, then choose a few that look tasty to you. Make two or three of those recipes this week so you can see how you can eat real food on keto. Eat as much as you want of those.

That's it for week 1. Seriously, that's it. No counting, no tracking, no worrying. Just do this all week and you'll be ready to take on week 2.

Week 2 Tips

Keep doing:

- You should already have given up grains, legumes/beans, and pasta/rice/potatoes.
- Enjoy your meat, veggies, nuts, cheese, cream, bacon, avocados, and other yummies as before.
- Find a few more keto-friendly recipes made with real food that sound good, and make two or three of them.

For week 2 you have three new goals:

1. *Reduce fruit* to once a day or better still, cut it out entirely. Cut out regular yogurt. You can use a little Greek yogurt if you must, but try to replace with a dab of sour cream instead.

2. *Start fasting between meals.* Go at least 4 hours between meals. Do not

eat snacks in between. So you could eat at 8 a.m., noon, 4 p.m., and 8 p.m., as an example. You need to keep insulin down. Eating causes insulin release. Insulin release = no fat burning. If you get super hungry, first drink water or a sugar-free beverage of choice. If that doesn't work, eat a fat bomb. This book is absolutely full of delicious fat bombs, many of which are no-cook, so finding a tasty fat bomb should not be difficult at all.

3. *Hydrate well.* Drink at least 64 ounces of liquid daily this week. Use it to hydrate, to fill your stomach in between meals, and to create a habit. Water really does help with fat loss.

That's it for week 2!

Week 3 Tips

Keep doing:

- You should already have given up grains, legumes/beans, and pasta/rice/potatoes.
- Enjoy your meat, veggies, nuts, cheese, cream, bacon, avocados, and other yummies as before.

- Find more keto-friendly recipes made with real food that sound good, and make two or three of them.
- Fast for 4 hours between meals.
- Hydrate well.

For week 3 you have three new goals:

1. *Cut out all fruit* except a handful of berries once a day. Over time you may be able to eat more, but this is a good start.

2. *Try 12-hour fasts.* You should already be fasting 4 hours between meals. Now go at least 12 hours between dinner and breakfast, or breakfast and lunch. Do not eat snacks in between. Eating causes insulin release. Insulin release = no fat burning. If you get super hungry, first drink water or a sugar-free beverage of choice. If that doesn't work, eat a fat bomb. This may sound daunting, but if you fast at night, you'll be asleep for 8 out of the 12 hours anyway, which may make it easier for you.

3. *Start tracking your food intake.* Find a food tracker you like and start keeping track of your carbs. Some options are MyFitnessPal, Lose It!, and Cronometer.

This week, you're not going to worry about balancing macros—simply focus on accurately tracking what you are eating.

Week 4 Tips

Keep doing:

- You should already have given up grains, legumes/beans, and pasta/rice/potatoes.
- Enjoy your meat, veggies, nuts, cheese, cream, bacon, avocados, and other yummies as before.
- Find more keto-friendly recipes made with real food that sound good, and make two or three new ones.
- Fast for 4 hours between meals.
- Hydrate well.
- Track your food using a good food tracker.

For week 4 you have three new goals:

1. *Educate yourself on macronutrients* and what foods contain carbs, fats, and proteins. Understanding and Calculating Macros on a Keto Diet (page 41) should be helpful. Calculate the appropriate macros for you by using the Keto Calculator on my website TwoSleevers.com (search for "Calculating Macros").

2. *Plan and track your daily intake* to ensure you are staying within the recommended macros. So yes, week 4 is the one where you finally start to track all your food. I know many others recommend starting out by tracking, but it can be absolutely overwhelming at first, and this is the main reason people hesitate to start keto. So I am asking you to hold off on tracking until you have weeks 1 to 3 under your belt and all is going well.

3. *Try intermittent fasting.* One to three times a week, try to go 14 to 16 hours between meals. Nothing you eat can increase insulin sensitivity or reduce insulin secretion as well as fasting can. Going longer between meals a few times a week can make a huge difference to health and to weight loss.

And that's it. Four weeks into it, you should be eating what you should, not eating when you shouldn't, tracking, losing weight, and feeling better. It really can be this simple.

Do consider joining my Facebook group for support, advice, and camaraderie—all of which can make a big difference when you're struggling. And we all struggle at times, no matter if keto is new or old hat. Finding like-minded people who can relate to your dilemmas can make all the difference on a difficult day.

UNDERSTANDING AND CALCULATING MACROS ON A KETO DIET

It's time for us to get a better understanding of macronutrients and why they matter. My aim here is to be accurate but not comprehensive. So I am going to simplify as best as I can.

Here are the topics we will cover:

- What are macronutrients?
- How many calories in carbohydrates/proteins/fat?
- Why do calories matter on a keto diet?
- What are the very basics of weight loss?
- What roles do macros play in insulin release?
- How do I calculate macros on a keto diet?
- What is the difference between total carbs and net carbs?
- Do calories matter on a keto diet?
- Do I have to eat all that fat on a keto diet?
- Do I need to adjust calories as I lose weight on a keto diet?
- So what's the bottom line?

WHAT ARE MACRONUTRIENTS?

For our purposes, macros (or macronutrients) are carbohydrates, protein, and fat (C/P/F). Any food can be thought of as a combination of C/P/F. Much of keto is maintaining the desirable balance between these macros, and for Keto Diet Plan Week 4 you need to understand this.

In a typical day on a keto diet plan, you want to eat between 20 and 50 grams of carbs, enough protein to maintain muscle mass, and enough fat to provide satiety.

Here's a high-level view of foods that contain a lot of carbs:

- **Starches** such as pasta, rice, potatoes, bread, oats
- **Sugars** such as sugar, honey, molasses, high-fructose corn syrup

- **Grains** such as quinoa, wheat, amaranth, millet
- **Beans and legumes** such as kidney beans, chickpeas, black-eyed peas (but not black soy beans)
- **Fruits,** especially tropical fruits (berries are lower-carb than other fruits)
- **Starchy vegetables** such as peas, corn, sweet potatoes, winter squash, etc.

HOW MANY CALORIES ARE IN CARBOHYDRATES/ PROTEINS/FAT?

Carbs and protein each have 4 calories per gram. Fat has 9 calories per gram.

WHY DO MACROS MATTER ON A KETO DIET PLAN?

There's a reason you are calculating macros: they serve as a proxy for things that will keep your insulin and blood sugar in check.

People argue endlessly about whether this ingredient or that "is keto." It's not an individual ingredient per se you should worry about—you should worry about being in ketosis. The ways to get into, and stay in, ketosis are:

- Control what you eat.
- Control when and how often you eat.

Let's talk about what you eat first, and the role macros play in this.

WHAT ARE THE VERY BASICS OF WEIGHT LOSS?

Here is what you need to know about weight loss in a nutshell (assuming your weight gain was related to excess consumption of carbohydrates, insulin resistance, excess appetite, and the like). You are either *FEASTING* (eating or having eaten within the last 2 to 4 hours) or you are *FASTING* (haven't eaten in a while). While you are feasting, your body is releasing insulin. While you have insulin in your bloodstream, you are not burning fat.

The way to burn fat is to a) not eat (i.e., fast) for long periods and b) eat foods that don't cause you to release excess insulin.

Feasting = Insulin

Insulin = No Fat Burning

Fasting = No Insulin

No Insulin = Fat Burning

Everything else about keto diets is just how to not release excess insulin so your body has a chance to burn fat. As I said earlier, the ways to do that are to a) control what you eat and b) control when and how often you eat.

WHAT ROLES DO MACROS PLAY IN INSULIN RELEASE?

Understand these three (oversimplified) facts, and you will understand how to eat for your keto diet plan:

- Carbs will make you release a *lot* of insulin.
- Protein, if eaten to excess, will make you release some insulin, but if you eat moderate amounts of protein you will be fine.
- Fat will not cause you to release insulin.

So the way to keep your insulin down? **Eat more fat, eat moderate protein, eat very few carbs, and go long periods without eating. That's it. No need to complicate things beyond this.**

Let's add that to our previous equations.

Feasting = Insulin

Carbs = Insulin

<u>Excess</u> Protein = Insulin

Insulin = No Fat Burning

Fasting = No Insulin

Fat = No Insulin

Low Carbs = Low Insulin

Moderate Protein = Low Insulin

No Insulin = Fat Burning

As I said earlier, it's an oversimplified view, but accurate nonetheless.

HOW DO I CALCULATE MACROS ON A KETO DIET PLAN?

Let's get this out of the way. There is no magic about the 20 grams of carbs everyone keeps pushing on keto. The right number of carbs is whatever will get you into ketosis and help you stay there. For some people that's 20 grams of carbs. For other people, it's 50 grams of carbs. The majority of us will reach ketosis at 20 grams of carbs if sustained over several days.

There are complicated ways to calculate macros. (And let's face it, I use the complicated ways that involve calculating lean body mass first, etc.) But we are going to keep it stupid simple for our Keto Diet Plan Week 4.

- You are going to get 20 grams of carbs.
- You are going to get 60 percent of your calories from fat.
- The rest of your calories will come from protein.

The easiest way to do this is to use a fitness calculator such as Cronometer or MyFitnessPal and let them do the calculations for you. You just specify 20 grams of carbs, 60% calories from fat, and the rest from protein.

If you insist on calculating it yourself, follow my logic below. If not, skip to the next section.

Remember that carbs and protein each have 4 calories per gram, and fat has 9 calories per gram.

Total calories. Start out by looking at the total calories you need. I won't repeat those calculations here since there are many reputable calculators out there. Let's say that you need 1,200 calories a day to lose weight.

Carbohydrate calories: We will assume you need 20 grams of carbs to be in ketosis.

20 grams $\times$ 4 calories $=$ 80 calories from carbs

This leaves you 1,110 calories to play with.

Fat Calories: 60 percent of your calories will come from fat.

1,200 $\times$ 60 percent (or .6) $=$ 720 calories

720 calories / 9 calories per gram $=$ 80 grams of fat

Protein Calories: The remainder of your calories will come from protein.

I have used up 80 carb calories + 720 fat calories, which leaves me 400 calories for protein.

400 calories / 4 calories per gram $=$ 100 grams of protein

WHAT IS THE DIFFERENCE BETWEEN TOTAL CARBS AND NET CARBS?

Net Carbs =
Total Carbs – Fiber – Sugar Alcohols

If you're diabetic, you may need to track total carbs. Many of the rest of us do well tracking net carbs, as fiber and sugar alcohols do not raise blood sugar or insulin levels for most people.

DO CALORIES MATTER ON A KETO DIET PLAN?

Yes, they do. Your body, much like me, is #lazyefficient. Given a choice, it will use energy from food to fuel itself. What you want is to make your body work to use its own body fat to fuel itself. This is a vastly oversimplified description of how your body works, but stay with me for a minute.

The way to make it use body fat to fuel itself is to keep insulin levels low and to not give it so much energy from food that it never needs to use body fat to fuel itself.

So, yes, calories do matter. But two things help. First, you will likely not be that hungry when eating a keto diet because you won't be crashing and burning from carb intake. Second, most people seem to be able to eat more (but not unlimited) calories on keto than on high-carb diets.

I will freely admit research on this is murky, and the usual calories in/calories out equations are not always backed by science. But I have yet to meet anyone who has eaten tons of calories and lost weight. If you can do that, more power to you. The rest of us schmucks need to track calories.

DO I HAVE TO EAT ALL THAT FAT ON A KETO DIET PLAN?

Here's what you need to know: Fat grams on keto are a limit, not a level. If you're hungry, eat fat. Remember:
fat = no insulin secretion = fat burning.

Personally, I feel that eating protein matters since it helps with maintaining muscle, and when you're losing weight, you do not want to lose muscle. So here's how I treat it:

Protein = Level and Limit. Hit the level and do not exceed the limit.

Carb = Limit. Do not exceed (but you don't have to eat to the limit).

Fat = Limit. Do not exceed (but you don't have to eat to the limit).

So eat fat to satiety. If you're hungry, eat all the fat grams your macros allot you. If you're not hungry, don't.

I eat all my protein. I keep carbs at 20 grams. I eat the fat specified. If I don't lose weight, I cut calories. Since I don't want to cut protein, I have to cut fat calories.

Then this puts my percentages out of whack, and all of a sudden I am consuming less fat as a percentage, and now I want to tear my hair out!

Except. I don't.

Those percentages? Nothing holy about them. They are merely heuristics. What matters is total insulin load and blood sugar swings. Because you know what? If I eat 20 grams of carbs, 100 grams of protein, and whatever fat I need to stay full while staying within my calorie limits?

I am. Doing. Just. Fine.

Even if my C/P/F percentages now look like 10/40/50 because I ate less fat that day, everything's okay. Stop worrying so much about details. Focus on the big picture: **Keep carbs low. Keep protein moderate. Eat mainly fat to keep yourself full. If you're in ketosis and not losing weight, cut calories.**

DO I NEED TO ADJUST MACROS AS I LOSE WEIGHT ON A KETO DIET PLAN?

You will need to adjust calories downward as you lose weight. The easy answer to this is that if you are losing weight, don't worry about readjusting so much. If you stop losing weight, it's time to tweak.

If you need to be more regimented, then after every 10 pounds or so of weight loss at first, readjust your calories. As you get closer your goal weight, you may have to adjust after every 5 pounds of weight loss. As you adjust calories, readjust your macros.

SO WHAT'S THE BOTTOM LINE?

Stop worrying so much about details. Again: Focus on the big picture. Keep carbs low. Keep protein moderate. Eat mainly fat to keep yourself full. If you're in ketosis and not losing weight, cut calories.

MINT CHOCOLATE BARS
page 147

GETTING BACK TO KETO BASICS

If you plan to adopt a ketogenic/low-carb way of eating for the rest of your life, there will definitely be times when you will fall off the wagon. In my case, that's usually off the wagon and facefirst into cupcakes. For those of us who follow keto for serious health issues, this can be dangerous, and the consequences are beyond my professional ability to discuss, so I won't touch those.

But for those of us who follow keto for weight loss/overall well-being reasons, I think this is not unusual. This happens to the best of us. The difficulty often is that one cupcake leads to another, followed by other high-carb things, and before you know it, you're slowly drifting back to your old, bad-for-you eating habits.

Over the last five years, I've definitely had to take myself in hand and get back on keto or low-carb again. Here are the ten ways in which I ensure that I can get back to keto:

Learn to distinguish real hunger from mouth hunger. We eat for a lot of reasons other than real hunger. You have to discover your own reasons for why you eat. I know I tend to munch if I'm happy or bored, and I am easily bored and often very happy, so that's a problem! I'm a lot less likely to eat mindlessly when stressed, so if I wanted to be skinny, I'd just have to stress myself out a lot. But I've found an easier and healthier way than this.

I've learned to distinguish between real hunger and mouth hunger, where I just want something good-tasting to munch on. I do this by asking myself two questions:

- Are you hungry enough to eat a piece of dry chicken breast? (which is the least exciting thing I can think of to eat). If the answer is yes, then I'm really hungry.
- Are you craving something in particular to eat? Or will you eat just about anything reasonable? If it's a particular craving, I'm not really hungry, I'm just wanting to munch.

If I'd eat just about anything reasonable, then I'm truly hungry. So when I say, "I need to eat something now," I'm really hungry. When I say to myself, "Let's see, what sounds good to eat?" Yeah, not really hungry then.

Go back to pre-planning and tracking. There's nothing worse than doing well all day and then discovering that you ate something that had a lot more carbs than you expected—and there goes your well-planned day. It's a lot easier to just plan what you're going to eat, enter it into your tracking app, and ensure that you will be on point if you follow the plan.

I find it also helps me to not have to worry all day about what to eat. It's already planned. I just have to eat it—which I am usually more than happy to do. Most of us have to track carbs and calories while on keto, and pre-planning helps with both.

Drink lots of liquids. Often when I think I'm hungry, the hunger goes away if I drink a little bit. In fact, for years I used what I called a "water loading" trick. An hour before I was scheduled to eat, I would drink a large glass of water. You'd be surprised how long you can feel full with a large glass of liquid sloshing about inside you.

Weigh all your food. After you've been doing this for a while, you may think you're pretty good at being able to guesstimate weight, but if you go over an ounce or two at each meal, that adds up to several hundred more calories than you should be eating. I also know that sometimes when I've gone back to weighing my food, I've been eating *less* than I should have because what I considered a 4-ounce piece of chicken actually turned out to only be 3 ounces. So weighing or measuring out your portions really helps you stay on track. It also introduces a discipline around meals that I may have lost when I fell off the wagon.

Fast between meals. *NO* grazing. This is critical on keto. Remember, you're trying to reduce insulin and reduce spikes in blood sugar. Nothing reduces insulin secretion as well as fasting. I usually set my clock to 4 hours between meals. If I get hungry within 3 or 4 hours of my last meal, I drink something instead, because it was really unlikely be real hunger. Not only does it limit calories, but it also reduces my insulin response. I have to remember that I am either feasting (eating) or fasting (going without food). And your body doesn't burn fat when feasting, so the longer I fast, the more I burn.

I usually set my clock for mealtimes to be 8 a.m., noon, 4 p.m., and a snack at 8 p.m. This also has the benefit of letting me fast for 12 hours overnight. You may prefer other times, but clock watching at first, when you have been eating at all times of day or night, is a good way to introduce some discipline into your life.

Identify carb levels for weight loss, for weight gain, and for maintenance, and then plan accordingly. In my case, I have to keep carbs below 20 to 40 grams for weight loss, and below 75 grams for maintenance. I am super carb-sensitive. While others can eat a lot more than 75 grams for maintenance (after all, 100 to 150 grams is considered low-carb by American standards), I didn't win the genetic lottery on this one.

You will have to experiment to find the appropriate levels for you, but once you know the levels, it makes planning a lot easier. Typically, I give myself two to three weeks at a particular level of carbs to see if I'm losing, gaining, or maintaining.

Eat more protein. Not eating enough protein is what got me in trouble in the first place. I'm a reluctant carnivore and would rather eat carbs than meat. But that doesn't work for me. I know keto is positioned as fat, fat, fat, and yes, eating fat to satiety is important—but so is protein. I try to get my protein in first and then "fill in around the edges" with fat. I also find that protein fills up my stomach really fast and stays with me for a really long time, so that's another reason I find it helpful to get my protein in daily, not just for overall muscle health but also for weight loss.

Accept hunger and don't think it needs to be fixed immediately. We believe that if we are hungry and don't eat, we will keep getting hungrier and hungrier until we just faint away like a Victorian lady. But most of us do not find that to be the case. Instead, hunger comes and goes in waves.

Often if I am hungry and I drink some-thing or distract myself with something or tell myself I need to wait for 2 more hours, the hunger goes away. The truth is, there's no way to lose weight without being hungry. Keto makes you less hungry than just restricting calories while continuing to eat carb-laden foods, but most of us have to learn to embrace the hunger. When I feel like I'm starving, I tell myself my body *must* be burning fat if I'm that ravenous, and that makes it easier to deal with.

Be patient. Rarely, if ever, have I lost more than a pound every other week. Sometimes I've stalled for 6 to 8 weeks.

So if I want to lose 10 pounds—the same 10 pounds that only took a week in Italy to jump onto my body—it could be close to 4 months before I can lose them. It's not fair, but it's my reality, so I just need to get into that medium- to long-term mind-set, rather than expecting miracles each time I get on the scale in the morning. This is easier said than done, I know, especially when the interwebz are full of people telling you how they lost 50 pounds in a month. I ~~hate~~ envy those people. But that is not how it works for me, and that is not how it works for thousands of other silent sufferers.

Allow yourself some treats so you don't feel deprived, but make them keto treats. This is where *Keto Fat Bombs, Sweets & Treats* comes in handy. What works for me is to have something planned and ready so that when the craving hits, I can grab a quick little keto treat and not feel deprived. Most of the recipes in this book also serve as fat bombs, so you will be satisfying your taste buds, your hunger, and your macros all in one fell and delicious swoop.

Okay, enough reading! Time to start cooking and eating. I wish you good health, and lovely meals—and lots of guilt-free desserts.

Coconut Flour

Shredded Coconut

Cocoa Powder

Almond Flour

Cornstarch

THE MAGNIFICENT SEVEN ESSENTIAL PANTRY INGREDIENTS FOR KETO DESSERTS AND BAKED GOODS

I wanted to write a keto cookbook that didn't require you to have eight different flour subs, four different sweeteners, and weird chemicals you can't pronounce, all just to make a little cake. So I have tried to limit the ingredients I use in this cookbook. Basically, if you have these seven things in addition to fresh ingredients, you should be able to make 90 percent of the recipes in this cookbook.

would desserts made with white flour. *Do not* interchange coconut flour and almond flour. They are not interchangeable at all. Don't write to me if you substitute one for the other and then your dessert doesn't work out. You've been warned ☺. You could try substituting other nut flours for almond flour, but you may have to tweak the recipes. I prefer to use superfine almond flour, which is called for throughout the book.

1. Superfine Almond Flour

This stalwart workhorse for keto baking is nutritious, delicious—and quite caloric. It is also quite filling, meaning you won't be able to eat as much of these desserts as you

2. Superfine Coconut Flour

Coconut flour is great for adding bulk and a little dryness and texture to a recipe. Coconut flour absorbs a lot of liquid, so a little goes a very long way. It's important to get superfine coconut flour, or you will have coconut shreds in your finished product.

I often get asked if products made with this flour taste like coconut. There could be a hint of coconut in the final taste, but it's not overpowering. As I mentioned above, you cannot interchange almond flour and coconut flour.

3. Chia Seeds

Chia seeds are so much fun and so versatile. Unless you're stuck in a time warp, you're probably not going to want to grow your own Chia Pet (although if you do, I'm not judging because they *are* kinda cute). Chia seeds great to help puddings gel, and they're fabulous for adding texture and crunch to breads. They absorb a lot of water and create some bulk in the recipe. People sometimes use chia gel instead of eggs.

They do add a little crunchiness to breads, so if you have picky eaters at home, you can do one of two things. Use white rather than black chia seeds so they are better hidden. You can also roughly grind them to make them a little smaller and less obvious. Note however, that if a recipe calls for chia seeds, they are not optional—they're essential to the recipe.

4. Swerve Sweetener, Granulated and Confectioners'

I know, I know, Swerve is expensive. I get it. Unfortunately for me, I'm one of those people who really has trouble with the taste of pure erythritol. Some of us get a cooling sensation with erythritol, and I can just taste it in recipes. Swerve, on the other hand, works really well for me. Since I have to taste all these recipes I make—sometimes several times until I get it right—I choose Swerve so I'm not suffering through the erythritol each time.

You can substitute erythritol if you like, but you will have to tweak the recipe and the amounts to adjust for sweetness. Since Swerve is expensive, I try to use it only for recipes where I feel that Truvía doesn't add sufficient bulk, which is typically in baked recipes.

5. Truvía or Splenda Sweetener

I use Truvía and powdered Splenda interchangeably for the most part. Truvía is basically stevia plus erythritol, and I like that it doesn't affect blood sugar, but also doesn't cost an arm and a leg.

6. Sugar-Free Chocolate Chips

There are many commercially available sugar-free chocolate chips. Unfortunately, some of them are sweetened with maltitol, which is almost as bad for you as refined white sugar. Try to find chips that are sweetened with stevia instead.

7. Xanthan Gum

I use this natural product as a thickener in place of cornstarch. Be very careful with how much you use since too much makes your final product . . . okay, there's no good way to say this . . . slimy. But in small quantities it's quite the workhorse, and I use it in soups, stews, ice creams, and puddings.

That's it for specialty ingredients used in this cookbook. How easy is that?

FRESH INGREDIENTS

Here are a few things that I always have on hand, not just for keto desserts, but for general keto cooking as well. The main reason I have them around, of course, is because they're delicious, versatile, and perfect for increasing your fat intake on keto.

- Cream cheese
- Butter
- Eggs
- Half-and-half
- Heavy cream
- Sour cream
- Almond milk
- Ricotta cheese
- Frozen berries

PANTRY INGREDIENTS

These are things you probably already have in your pantry:

- Baking soda
- Baking powder
- Unsweetened cocoa powder
- Full-fat canned coconut milk
- Coconut oil
- Keto-friendly cooking spray, made with coconut oil, avocado oil, or ghee
- Various extracts such as pure vanilla, orange, lemon, almond, etc.
- Peanut butter
- Sugar-free flavored gelatin
- Unflavored powdered gelatin
- Ground cinnamon
- Ground nutmeg

Sunflower Seeds

Dried Cranberries

Almonds

Pecans

Pumpkin Seeds

Cashews

BREADS

ALMOND-ORANGE SCONES

Don't let appearances fool you on this one. They may not look exactly like the scones at your favorite coffee shop (which, FYI, typically have more than 60 grams of carbs each!), but they taste fantastic. You can, of course, vary the flavors to suit your tastes.

ACTIVE TIME: 15 minutes

TOTAL TIME: 50 minutes

SERVINGS: 8

DIETARY CONSIDERATIONS

Vegetarian

MACROS

83% Fat

7% Carbs

10% Protein

PER SERVING

Calories: 220

Total Fat: 20g

Total Carbs: 17g

Net Carbs: 4g

Fiber: 3g

Sugar: 1g

Protein: 5g

FOR THE SCONES

1 cup superfine almond flour

¼ cup superfine coconut flour

¼ cup Swerve granulated sweetener

1 teaspoon baking powder

¼ teaspoon sea salt

1 large egg

¼ cup heavy cream

4 tablespoons (½ stick) unsalted butter, melted

1 teaspoon orange extract

¼ cup slivered almonds

FOR THE GLAZE

1 tablespoon full-fat cream cheese

1 tablespoon unsalted butter

3 tablespoons Swerve granulated sweetener

1. For the scones: Preheat the oven to 350°F. Line a baking sheet with parchment paper; set aside.

2. In a large bowl, whisk together the almond flour, coconut flour, sweetener, baking powder, and salt. Make a well in the dry ingredients.

3. Add the egg and beat in the well. Pour in the cream, melted butter, and orange extract and stir until smooth. Stir in the slivered almonds.

4. Place the dough on the prepared baking sheet. Pat into a 6-inch-diameter, ½-inch-thick loaf. Cut into 8 wedges and separate the wedges slightly so they don't bake together.

continued...

5. Bake for 25 minutes, or until golden. Turn off the oven and leave the scones in the oven for 10 to 15 minutes.

6. For the glaze: Combine the cream cheese, butter, and sweetener in a microwave-safe bowl. Microwave on high for 30 seconds. Mix well with a fork until the butter and cream cheese have melted and the mixture is smooth. (If necessary, microwave in 10-second increments, stirring between each, until smooth.)

7. Drizzle the glaze over the scones. Serve warm.

CHOCOLATE CHIP COOKIES
page 105

CRANBERRY CHOCOLATE BARK
page 141

COCONUT MACAROONS
page 123

BASIC PANCAKES

Everyone needs a good, basic pancake recipe in their repertoire, so here you go. You can make these sweet, or go savory by leaving out the sweetener. They're great as wraps or just as pancakes, of course. A little sugar-free maple syrup, a lot of butter, and you're all set.

Keto cooking spray

2 cups superfine blanched almond flour

½ cup superfine coconut flour

⅓ cup Swerve granulated sweetener

2 teaspoons baking powder

10 large eggs

½ cup water

8 tablespoons solid coconut oil or unsalted butter (1 stick), melted

1 tablespoon vanilla extract

1. Grease an electric griddle with cooking spray and preheat to 375°F (or heat 2 tablespoons coconut oil in a large nonstick skillet over medium heat).

2. In a large bowl, combine the almond flour, coconut flour, sweetener, baking powder, eggs, water, melted coconut oil, and vanilla. Whisk until well combined.

3. In batches and using ¼ cup of batter per pancake, pour batter onto the griddle. Cook until the surfaces of the pancakes are bubbling, 2 to 3 minutes. Turn and cook on the other sides until cooked through, 1 to 2 minutes. Repeat to cook the remaining batter. Serve warm.

ACTIVE TIME: 25 minutes

TOTAL TIME: 25 minutes

SERVINGS: 10 (1 PANCAKE EACH)

DIETARY CONSIDERATIONS
Dairy-Free
Vegetarian

MACROS
77% Fat
6% Carbs
14% Protein

PER SERVING
Calories: 336
Total Fat: 29g
Total Carbs: 15g
Net Carbs: 5g
Fiber: 4g
Sugar: 2g
Protein: 12g

BLUEBERRY SOUR CREAM MUFFINS

I've always loved a good muffin. But I loved them a lot less after I realized that they were not as healthy as I had thought. So I made these blueberry muffins to satisfy my craving. It's a great base recipe that you can change to suit your taste—or what's in your fridge. Be sure to use a light hand when mixing the blueberries—unless you want Smurf-colored muffins!

Keto cooking spray

¼ cup superfine coconut flour

½ teaspoon baking powder

¼ cup Swerve granulated sweetener

3 large eggs

¼ cup full-fat sour cream

1 teaspoon almond extract

1 cup fresh blueberries

1. Preheat the oven to 350°F. Lightly grease a 6-cup muffin pan with cooking spray (or line it with silicone cupcake liners); set aside.

2. In a medium bowl, combine the coconut flour, baking powder, and sweetener. Stir well to combine. Make a well in the dry ingredients. Add the eggs and beat lightly in the well. Add the sour cream and almond extract and stir to make a smooth batter. Gently fold in the blueberries. Divide the batter evenly among the prepared muffin cups.

3. Bake the muffins for 20 to 25 minutes, until the tops have browned. Cool for about 5 minutes in the pan, then transfer to a wire rack to cool completely.

ACTIVE TIME: 10 minutes

TOTAL TIME: 35 minutes

SERVINGS: 6

DIETARY CONSIDERATIONS

Vegetarian

MACROS

59% Fat

19% Carbs

16% Protein

PER SERVING

Calories: 107

Total Fat: 7g

Total Carbs: 15g

Net Carbs: 5g

Fiber: 2g

Sugar: 3g

Protein: 4g

CAULIFLOWER BREAD STICKS

Is there no end to the creative ways to use cauliflower? Apparently not! These bread sticks are great for non-keto eaters as well, and as the mom of a picky eater, I was delighted that I was able to sneak some veggies into my unsuspecting son. These are best eaten hot, although they reheat rather well.

2 large eggs

2 cups riced cauliflower

1 teaspoon Italian seasoning

½ teaspoon granulated garlic

½ teaspoon kosher salt

½ teaspoon ground black pepper

1 cup shredded mozzarella or Mexican cheese blend

¼ cup grated Parmesan cheese

ACTIVE TIME: 15 minutes

TOTAL TIME: 50 minutes

SERVINGS: 8

DIETARY CONSIDERATIONS
Vegetarian

MACROS
59% Fat
5% Carbs
33% Protein

PER SERVING
Calories: 76
Total Fat: 5g
Total Carbs: 2g
Net Carbs: 1g
Fiber: 1g
Sugar: 1g
Protein: 6g

1. Preheat the oven to 350°F. Line a large rimmed baking sheet with parchment paper (or generously grease with olive oil or butter); set aside.

2. In a blender or food processor, combine the eggs, cauliflower, Italian seasoning, granulated garlic, salt, pepper, and mozzarella cheese. Blend or process on low speed until the ingredients are well incorporated and the cauliflower has broken down further.

3. Transfer the cauliflower mixture to the prepared pan and pat it into a rectangle about ¼ inch thick.

4. Bake for 30 minutes. Remove from the oven and sprinkle the top with the Parmesan cheese. Turn the broiler to high. Broil for 2 to 3 minutes, until the Parmesan cheese is melted and golden brown.

5. Let cool slightly, then slice into 8 breadsticks.

COTTAGE CHEESE DOLLAR PANCAKES

Take the "dollar" part of this recipe seriously. The pancakes are best when you make little ones, as the big ones tend to fall apart a bit. But if you follow the directions, you'll have some fantastic little pancakes. And let's face it, they're so cute when they're little! (If you are looking for thicker, sturdier pancakes, try the Basic Pancakes recipe on page 69.)

ACTIVE TIME: 15 minutes

TOTAL TIME: 15 minutes

SERVINGS: 2 (4 PANCAKES EACH)

DIETARY CONSIDERATIONS
Vegetarian

MACROS
68% Fat
6% Carbs
25% Protein

PER SERVING
Calories: 312
Total Fat: 23g
Total Carbs: 19g
Net Carbs: 5g
Fiber: 2g
Sugar: 2g
Protein: 19g

3 large eggs

½ cup full-fat cottage cheese

⅓ cup superfine blanched almond flour

¼ cup unsweetened almond milk

2 tablespoons Swerve granulated sweetener

½ teaspoon vanilla extract

1 teaspoon baking powder

Solid coconut oil, butter, or nonstick cooking spray

1. In a blender, combine the eggs, cottage cheese, almond flour, almond milk, sweetener, vanilla, and baking powder. Blend until the mixture is smooth.

2. Heat a nonstick skillet over medium-high heat. Add a little coconut oil or butter to the pan (or spray with cooking spray) and heat until the fat is bubbling. In batches and using 2 tablespoons of the batter per pancake, pour the batter into the pan. (This is a very liquid and delicate batter—don't try to make large pancakes, as they will not flip over easily.) Cook until bubbles appear and then disappear on the tops of the pancakes, 1 to 2 minutes. Gently loosen the pancakes with a spatula and flip. Cook for an additional 30 seconds to 1 minute, until golden brown.

3. Repeat with the remaining batter. Serve the pancakes hot.

DRIED-FRUIT SCUFFINS

This is one of the few instances where I use a ready-made mix like Carbquick. The dried fruit may not be strictly keto. But I created this one Christmas when I was dying for fruitcake (I love fruitcake, OK??). While not strictly keto unless you do IIFYM, it's a lot better for me than fruitcake. Soaking and draining the fruit reduces the sugar a little. You can use berries or nuts instead.

ACTIVE TIME: 15 minutes

TOTAL TIME: 1 hour 30 minutes

SERVINGS: 12

DIETARY CONSIDERATIONS

Vegetarian

MACROS

62% Fat

29% Carbs

9% Protein

PER SERVING

Calories: 168

Total Fat: 12g

Total Carbs: 20g

Net Carbs: 12g

Fiber: 8g

Sugar: 5g

Protein: 4g

¾ cup chopped no-sugar-added mixed dried fruit

Keto cooking spray

4 tablespoons (½ stick) unsalted butter, cut into large chunks

2 cups Carbquik baking mix

1 large egg

½ cup heavy cream

1 teaspoon almond extract

⅓ cup Swerve granulated sweetener

1. Soak the fruit in hot water for 1 hour to soften. Drain the fruit in a strainer for 15 minutes.

2. Preheat the oven to 375°F. Generously grease a large baking sheet with cooking spray; set aside.

3. In a medium bowl, combine the butter and baking mix. Using a pastry cutter, cut the butter into the mix until the mixture has the texture of small peas.

4. In a small bowl, combine the egg, cream, almond extract, and sweetener. Whisk until combined. Add to the dry mixture and stir until well blended.

5. Fold in the rehydrated mixed fruit. Form the mixture into 12 balls and place on the prepared baking sheet. Push down to flatten slightly and neaten the edges.

6. Bake for 15 to 20 minutes, until the tops are browned and a toothpick inserted into the center of one of the scuffins comes out clean.

LEMON-POPPY SEED MUFFINS

Ricotta, lemon, and poppy seeds make a lovely combination for a moist, delicious little muffin. Once again, treat this as a base muffin recipe that you can change up to suit whatever you're craving that day.

ACTIVE TIME: 10 minutes

TOTAL TIME: 50 minutes

SERVINGS: 12

DIETARY CONSIDERATIONS

Vegetarian

MACROS

83% Fat

5% Carbs

12% Protein

PER SERVING

Calories: 146

Total Fat: 13g

Total Carbs: 8g

Net Carbs: 2g

Fiber: 8g

Sugar: 5g

Protein: 5g

1 cup superfine blanched almond flour

3 large eggs

⅓ cup Swerve granulated sweetener

¼ cup whole-milk ricotta cheese

¼ cup solid coconut oil

¼ cup heavy cream

4 packets True Lemon crystallized lemon

2 tablespoons poppy seeds

1 teaspoon baking powder

1 teaspoon lemon extract

1. Preheat the oven to 350°F. Line a 12-cup muffin pan with paper cupcake liners.

2. In a large bowl, combine the almond flour, eggs, sweetener, ricotta cheese, coconut oil, cream, crystallized lemon, poppy seeds, baking powder, and lemon extract. Beat with an electric mixer on medium until fluffy.

3. Divide the batter evenly among the lined muffin cups.

4. Bake for 40 minutes, or until a toothpick inserted into the center of one of the muffins comes out clean.

5. Cool slightly before removing the liners.

RECIPE NOTES

You can also use 1 tablespoon fresh lemon juice plus the zest of 1 lemon instead of True Lemon packets.

NUT & SEED BREAD

I know this seems like an odd recipe, but it really does work. It's not eggy, it slices and freezes beautifully, and it is very filling. You can use salted or unsalted nuts, adjusting the salt you add accordingly. Use a combination of large nuts (left whole) and seeds. The flaxseed is critical for holding the mixture together. Make up a loaf, slice once cooled, freeze some for later, and eat the rest with lots of butter and maybe some Mixed Berry Jam (page 223).

Keto cooking spray

½ cup flaxseeds

½ cup unsalted raw pistachios

½ cup unsalted raw almonds

½ cup unsalted raw walnuts

½ cup unsalted raw cashews

½ cup sesame seeds

3 large eggs, lightly beaten

¼ cup melted coconut oil, plus additional for greasing the pan

½ teaspoon salt

1. Preheat the oven to 325°F. Grease an 8×4-inch loaf pan with cooking spray.

2. In a large bowl, combine the flaxseeds, pistachios, almonds, walnuts, cashews, sesame seeds, eggs, oil, and salt. Stir until well combined. Transfer the mixture to the greased pan.

3. Bake for 45 minutes. Cool the bread in the pan on a wire rack for 10 minutes. Turn the bread out of the pan and let it cool completely on the wire rack before slicing.

> ### RECIPE NOTES
>
> *You can use whatever combination of nuts and seeds you like, as long as it adds up to 3 cups. The only ingredient you really need to include are the flaxseeds (or ground flax) to bind the ingredients. A mix of big nuts and small seeds gives an interesting texture to the bread.*

ACTIVE TIME: 15 minutes

TOTAL TIME: 1 hour 10 minutes

SERVINGS: 12 (1 SLICE EACH)

DIETARY CONSIDERATIONS

Dairy-Free

Vegetarian

MACROS

81% Fat

6% Carbs

12% Protein

PER SERVING

Calories: 258

Total Fat: 23g

Total Carbs: 8g

Net Carbs: 4g

Fiber: 4g

Sugar: 1g

Protein: 8g

SANDWICH BREAD
page 82

SANDWICH BREAD

Let me tell you something. It is *not* easy to make a keto bread, especially one that is not eggy. I tried many, many different varieties before I settled on this. It is best eaten at room temperature, so be patient and try not to scarf it down when it's still hot. You can use either black chia seeds, which show up in the slices, or white ones, which tend to disappear into the bread. It also makes really good keto French toast the next day.

Keto cooking spray

4 large eggs, lightly beaten

1 cup superfine blanched almond flour

½ cup chia seeds

¼ cup unsweetened almond milk or water

4 tablespoons solid coconut oil or butter (½ stick), melted

2 teaspoons baking soda

½ teaspoon salt

ACTIVE TIME: 10 minutes

TOTAL TIME: 50 minutes

SERVINGS: 6
(2 SLICES EACH)

DIETARY CONSIDERATIONS
Dairy-Free
Vegetarian

MACROS
80% Fat
2% Carbs
15% Protein

PER SERVING
Calories: 336
Total Fat: 30g
Total Carbs: 11g
Net Carbs: 4g
Fiber: 9g
Sugar: 1g
Protein: 12g

1. Preheat the oven to 350°F. Grease an 8×4-inch loaf pan with cooking spray; set aside. (Do not use a larger loaf pan or the bread will be very flat.)

2. In a large bowl, combine the eggs, almond flour, chia seeds, almond milk, melted coconut oil, baking soda, and salt. Stir until well combined and no lumps remain.

3. Pour the batter into the prepared pan and bake for 30 minutes. Cool the bread in the pan on a wire rack for 10 minutes. Turn the bread out of the pan. Let cool completely before serving.

SEED CRACKERS

One of the hardest things about keto for a beginner is giving up on crunchy things. I often use cheese chips that I make at home to satisfy the crunch. But sometimes, you just want crackers—preferably with cheese. These take a while to bake, but they keep well in a covered tin. So make up a batch and munch on!

Keto cooking spray

2 cups cool water

3 tablespoons psyllium husk powder

2 cups mixed seeds (See Notes)

1. Preheat the oven to 350°F. Generously grease a 14×16-inch rimmed baking sheet with cooking spray (or line it with a silicone baking mat).

2. Pour the water into a large bowl. Gradually add the psyllium husk powder, whisking constantly. (Do not use hot water or add the water to the powder.) When all the lumps have dissolved, add the salt and seeds, stirring well to combine. Depending on your husk powder, you may need to add a few more seeds, but before you do that, let the mixture rest for 10 to 15 minutes. This gives the psyllium a chance to gel.

3. Once the mixture has gelled, spread it as thinly and evenly as you can over the prepared pan. (To reduce stickiness, occasionally dip your fingers in a bowl of cool water.)

continued...

ACTIVE TIME: 20 minutes

TOTAL TIME: 1 hour 15 minutes

SERVINGS: 8 (4 CRACKERS EACH)

DIETARY CONSIDERATIONS
Egg-Free
Dairy-Free
Vegan

MACROS
74% Fat
6% Carbs
14% Protein

PER SERVING
Calories: 250
Total Fat: 20g
Total Carbs: 12g
Net Carbs: 4g
Fiber: 8g
Sugar: 1g
Protein: 9g

4. Bake for 30 minutes. Use a pizza cutter or a sharp knife to score (not cut) the sheet into 32 crackers. Put the pan back in the oven and bake for 15 minutes more.

5. Remove the pan from the oven and allow the crackers to cool completely to crisp up, 45 to 60 minutes.

6. Break the crackers along the scored lines. Store in a tightly sealed container for up to 2 weeks.

RECIPE NOTES

You can vary the seed combination in the recipe as long as you have 2 cups total. Try 1 cup sunflower seeds + ½ cup pumpkin seeds + ¼ cup flaxseeds + ¼ cup sesame seeds.

SAVORY CHEESE MUFFINS

I love savory muffins so very much. They're great for a quick breakfast, but also good alongside a bowl of soup or just as a quick snack when you're running around. This base recipe can be adapted many different ways. My favorite variation is bacon and chives.

Keto cooking spray

1 cup superfine blanched almond flour

½ cup chia seeds

2 teaspoons baking powder

½ teaspoon granulated garlic

4 large eggs

4 tablespoons (½ stick) butter, melted

¼ cup heavy cream

½ cup grated cheddar cheese

ACTIVE TIME: 10 minutes
TOTAL TIME: 55 minutes
SERVINGS: 12

DIETARY CONSIDERATIONS
Vegetarian

MACROS
80% Fat
4% Carbs
15% Protein

PER SERVING
Calories: 198
Total Fat: 18g
Total Carbs: 6g
Net Carbs: 2g
Fiber: 4g
Sugar: 1g
Protein: 7g

1. Preheat the oven to 350°F. Grease a 12-cup muffin pan with cooking spray (or line it with silicone cupcake liners); set aside

2. In a medium bowl, combine the almond flour, chia seeds, baking powder, and granulated garlic. Make a well in the dry ingredients. Add the eggs and beat in the well, then pour in the melted butter and cream. Stir until smooth. Gently fold in the cheese.

3. Divide the batter evenly among the prepared muffin cups. Bake for 35 to 40 minutes, until the tops are well browned. Turn off the oven and leave the muffins in the oven for 10 to 15 minutes. Serve warm.

VARIATIONS

ROSEMARY-CHEESE MUFFINS

Add 1 teaspoon dried rosemary with the granulated garlic.

HAM & CHEESE MUFFINS

Omit the cheddar cheese. Instead, fold in ¼ cup grated Swiss cheese and ¼ cup diced ham.

BACON & CHIVE MUFFINS

Omit the cheddar cheese. Instead, fold in ¼ cup crumbled cooked bacon and ¼ cup chopped fresh chives.

ZUCCHINI BREAD

I made this bread in a pretty swirly Bundt pan and got rave reviews for it. Based on feedback from testers, if you're using zucchini that is particularly "juicy," you may want to let it drain in a colander, then squeeze out excess water before you mix the zucchini into the batter.

Keto cooking spray

½ cup Swerve granulated sweetener

3 large eggs

½ cup melted coconut oil or ghee

1½ cups superfine blanched almond flour

½ cup superfine coconut flour

1 teaspoon baking powder

1 teaspoon baking soda

½ teaspoon ground cinnamon

¼ teaspoon ground nutmeg

½ cup unsweetened almond milk

2 cups shredded zucchini

1 cup chopped walnuts

ACTIVE TIME: 20 minutes

TOTAL TIME: 1 hour 10 minutes

SERVINGS: 8

DIETARY CONSIDERATIONS

Dairy-Free

Vegetarian

MACROS

84% Fat

6% Carbs

10% Protein

PER SERVING

Calories: 415

Total Fat: 39g

Total Carbs: 24g

Net Carbs: 6g

Fiber: 6g

Sugar: 2g

Protein: 10g

1. Preheat the oven to 350°F. Grease a 6-cup Bundt pan with cooking spray; set aside.

2. In the bowl of a stand mixer fitted with the paddle attachment, combine the sweetener, eggs, and the ½ cup oil or ghee and beat until the ingredients are fluffy, 2 to 3 minutes.

3. Add the almond flour, coconut flour, baking powder, baking soda, cinnamon, nutmeg, and almond milk. Beat for an additional 2 to 3 minutes.

4. Remove the bowl from the stand mixer. Stir in the zucchini and walnuts. Pour the mixture into the prepared pan and spread it evenly.

5. Bake for 50 minutes, or until a toothpick inserted into the middle of the cake comes out clean. Cool completely on a wire rack before serving.

CAKES, COOKIES & BROWNIES

CINNAMON MUG CAKE

For years I avoided mug cakes because I am an absolute cake fiend. I mean I *looove* cake. So I knew if I made a good mug cake, I'd be in trouble. This is a good mug cake. I have had to hide the recipe from myself. Seriously.

1 large egg

1 tablespoon heavy cream

¼ teaspoon vanilla extract

⅓ cup superfine bleached almond flour

1 tablespoon plus 1 teaspoon Swerve granulated sweetener

¼ teaspoon ground cinnamon

½ teaspoon baking powder

1. In a large coffee mug, beat together the egg, cream, and vanilla. Add the almond flour, sweetener, cinnamon, and baking powder. Stir until well combined and no lumps remain.

2. Microwave on high for 1 minute, or until the cake has pulled away from the sides and the top is set but still moist.

3. Cool for 5 minutes before serving.

ACTIVE TIME: 10 minutes

TOTAL TIME: 16 minutes

SERVINGS: 1

DIETARY CONSIDERATIONS

Vegetarian

MACROS

76% Fat

6% Carbs

17% Protein

PER SERVING

Calories: 338

Total Fat: 29g

Total Carbs: 25g

Net Carbs: 5g

Fiber: 4g

Sugar: 2g

Protein: 15g

5-INGREDIENT FLOURLESS BROWNIES

I love these brownies, but I worry a little about how easy they are to make. You could bake them in a round pan, like a flourless cake, or you could bake them in a square one and cut them into squares—keeping the lovely edge pieces for yourself. This easy recipe is definitely a go-to in my house.

ACTIVE TIME: 10 minutes

TOTAL TIME: 40 minutes

SERVINGS: 6

DIETARY CONSIDERATIONS
Vegetarian

MACROS
80% Fat
3% Carbs
6% Protein

PER SERVING
Calories: 274
Total Fat: 25g
Total Carbs: 20g
Net Carbs: 2g
Fiber: 1g
Sugar: 0g
Protein: 4g

Keto cooking spray

½ cup sugar-free chocolate chips

8 tablespoons (1 stick) unsalted butter

3 large eggs

¼ cup Swerve granulated sweetener

1 teaspoon vanilla extract

Whipped cream (optional)

1. Preheat the oven to 350°F. Grease a 6-inch springform pan or cake pan with cooking spray; set aside.

2. In a medium microwave-safe bowl, combine the chocolate chips and butter. Microwave on high for 1 minute, stopping and stirring once. Remove from the microwave and stir until all lumps have melted into the mixture (don't continue to microwave the mixture).

3. In a large bowl, combine the eggs, sweetener, and vanilla. Whisk until light and frothy. Slowly pour the melted chocolate mixture into the bowl, whisking until well blended.

4. Pour the batter into the prepared pan. Bake for 30 minutes, or until a toothpick inserted into the center of the brownie comes out clean.

5. Serve with whipped cream, if desired.

SPANISH ALMENDRADOS COOKIES

I love when a traditional recipe already uses keto-friendly ingredients. These little morsels are traditionally made with almond flour, so it was but the work of a moment to adapt them to be keto-compliant. The little almond on top is optional but very festive looking.

1 large egg

1½ cups superfine blanched almond flour

⅓ to ½ cup Swerve granulated sweetener

1 teaspoon lemon extract

1 tablespoon grated lemon zest

24 whole blanched almonds (optional)

ACTIVE TIME: 20 minutes

TOTAL TIME: 1 hour 45 minutes

SERVINGS: 12 (2 COOKIES EACH)

DIETARY CONSIDERATIONS
Dairy-Free
Vegetarian

MACROS
76% Fat
7% Carbs
16% Protein

PER SERVING
Calories: 107
Total Fat: 9g
Total Carbs: 9g
Net Carbs: 2g
Fiber: 2g
Sugar: 1g
Protein: 4g

1. In a medium bowl, beat the egg. Add the almond flour, sweetener, lemon extract, and lemon zest. Stir until well blended. Cover and chill in the refrigerator for 1 to 2 hours.

2. Preheat the oven to 350°F. Line a baking sheet with parchment paper.

3. Pinch off 24 walnut-size pieces of dough and roll into balls. Gently press an almond on top of each ball and arrange them 1 inch apart on the lined baking sheet.

4. Bake until the cookies have the barest hint of color but remain soft, 18 to 20 minutes. Cool on the pan on a wire rack for 5 minutes, then remove from the pan and cool completely on the rack. Store in an airtight container.

ALMOND SHORTBREAD

Crunchy, buttery, not too sweet—and so easy to make. This simple little short-bread can be served for dessert, but also used as a prebaked pie crust. The squares keep well for up to a week if covered—although you may not be able to resist eating them all before then.

Keto cooking spray

4 tablespoons (½ stick) unsalted butter, softened

½ to ⅔ cup Swerve granulated sweetener

2 teaspoons almond extract

1 cup superfine blanched almond flour

ACTIVE TIME: 15 minutes

TOTAL TIME: 45 minutes

SERVINGS: 8

DIETARY CONSIDERATIONS

Egg-Free

Vegetarian

MACROS

85% Fat

3% Carbs

8% Protein

PER SERVING

Calories: 147

Total Fat: 14g

Total Carbs: 15g

Net Carbs: 1g

Fiber: 2g

Sugar: 1g

Protein: 3g

1. Preheat the oven to 350°F. Lightly grease an 8-inch square baking pan with cooking spray; set aside.

2. In the bowl of a stand mixer fitted with the paddle attachment, combine the butter and sweetener. Beat on medium speed until fluffy, 3 to 4 minutes. Add the almond extract and beat until blended, about 30 seconds. Gradually add the almond flour and beat on low until well blended, about 2 minutes.

3. Transfer the dough to the prepared pan. Pat it lightly to even out the thickness. Bake for 30 minutes, or until the top starts to lightly brown.

4. Remove the pan from the oven and cut the shortbread into 8 pieces while it is still warm and soft. Cool completely in the pan on a wire rack before serving.

ALMOND-COCONUT-BLUEBERRY CAKELETS

Keto desserts are delicious, but they can be caloric. I like making little cakes when a small bite is all I need. Be careful to not overmix the batter and break the blueberries, otherwise you will have blue Smurf cakes. You can of course substitute a different berry for the blueberries.

Keto cooking spray

3 large eggs

1 cup superfine blanched almond flour

⅓ cup heavy cream

⅓ cup Swerve granulated sweetener

¼ cup unsweetened shredded coconut

¼ cup coconut oil or unsalted butter (½ stick), melted

1 teaspoon baking powder

½ teaspoon almond extract

¼ cup frozen wild blueberries, thawed

1. Preheat the oven to 350°F. Grease a mini-muffin pan with cooking spray (or line it with silicone mini-cupcake liners).

2. In a blender, combine the eggs, almond flour, cream, sweetener, shredded coconut, coconut oil, baking powder, and almond extract. Blend until light and frothy. Pour the mixture into a medium bowl and gently stir in the blueberries.

3. Divide the batter among the prepared muffin cups.

4. Bake for 35 minutes, or until a toothpick inserted into the center of a cakelet comes out clean.

5. Cool completely in the pan on a wire rack before unmolding.

ACTIVE TIME: 15 minutes

TOTAL TIME: 50 minutes

SERVINGS: 12 (2 CAKELETS EACH)

DIETARY CONSIDERATIONS

Vegetarian

MACROS

85% Fat

5% Carbs

10% Protein

PER SERVING

Calories: 153

Total Fat: 15g

Total Carbs: 8g

Net Carbs: 7g

Fiber: 2g

Sugar: 1g

Protein: 4g

BUTTERY ALMOND POUND CAKE

This recipe makes a much larger cake than my other recipes, so it's definitely a good party cake since there will be enough to share. As written, the recipe isn't very sweet. If you want it slightly sweeter, increase the Swerve or Truvía. Be sure to beat the batter well so that you have a good crumb. It does really well when toasted the next day too. Many people in my TwoSleevers Facebook group made a lemon pound cake out of this (see Note), so feel free to experiment!

ACTIVE TIME: 15 minutes

TOTAL TIME: 1 hour 5 minutes

SERVINGS: 8

DIETARY CONSIDERATIONS

Vegetarian

MACROS

83% Fat

5% Carbs

13% Protein

PER SERVING

Calories: 326

Total Fat: 30g

Total Carbs: 25g

Net Carbs: 4g

Fiber: 3g

Sugar: 2g

Protein: 10g

FOR THE CAKE

Keto cooking spray

4 ounces full-fat cream cheese, softened

4 tablespoons (½ stick) unsalted butter, softened

¾ cup Swerve granulated sweetener

1 teaspoon almond extract

4 large eggs

¼ cup full-fat sour cream

2 cups superfine blanched almond flour

2 teaspoons baking powder

TO GARNISH (OPTIONAL)

Mixed fresh berries

Whipped cream

1. For the cake: Preheat the oven to 350°F. Grease a 6-cup Bundt pan or large loaf pan with cooking spray; set aside.

2. In the bowl of a stand mixer fitted with the paddle attachment, combine the cream cheese, butter, and sweetener and beat until the mixture is light and fluffy and the ingredients are well blended.

3. Add the almond extract and mix. Add the eggs and sour cream and mix. Add the almond flour and baking powder and beat until all the ingredients are well blended and the batter is light and fluffy.

continued...

4. Pour the batter into the prepared pan. Bake for 40 minutes, or until a toothpick inserted into the center of the cake comes out clean.

5. Cool in the pan on a wire rack for 10 minutes. Remove from the pan and cool completely on the rack. If desired, serve with fresh berries and whipped cream.

VARIATION

LEMON POUND CAKE

Substitute lemon extract for the almond extract and add 1 tablespoon grated lemon zest along with the extract.

CHOCOLATE CHIP COOKIES

The only thing you need to know before you make these cookies is that you want to flatten them out so they cook evenly—and that you won't be able to eat just one. They spread only just a little, so be sure you're not putting large, round scoops of dough down. In the end, the testers all agreed that these taste as close to the sugared version as you will get.

ACTIVE TIME: 20 minutes
TOTAL TIME: 40 minutes
SERVINGS: 12
(2 COOKIES EACH)

DIETARY CONSIDERATIONS
Vegetarian

MACROS
78% Fat
6% Carbs
7% Protein

PER SERVING
Calories: 287
Total Fat: 25g
Total Carbs: 24g
Net Carbs: 4g
Fiber: 3g
Sugar: 1g
Protein: 5g

Keto cooking spray

8 tablespoons (1 stick) unsalted butter

½ cup Swerve granulated sweetener

1 large egg

1½ cups superfine blanched almond flour

1 teaspoon baking powder

½ teaspoon salt

1 teaspoon vanilla extract

1 cup sugar-free chocolate chips

½ cup chopped nuts

1. Preheat the oven to 350°F. Grease a large baking sheet with cooking spray; set aside.

2. In the bowl of a stand mixer fitted with the paddle attachment, combine the butter and sweetener and beat until smooth. Add the egg and beat until combined. Add the flour, baking powder, salt, and vanilla. Mix until the ingredients are well combined. Fold in the chocolate chips and nuts.

3. Drop by heaping tablespoons onto the prepared baking sheet in 12 portions and flatten each slightly. Bake until firm and lightly golden but not browned, 14 to 15 minutes.

4. Cool on the pan on a wire rack for 5 minutes, then remove from the pan and cool completely on the rack. Store in an airtight container.

CREAM CHEESE COOKIES

Just the name will tell you all you need to know. They're cookies. They have cream cheese. They're delicious. What more do you need to hear before you run to the kitchen and make them? Perfect with a cup of tea or coffee. Let them cool so they firm up a bit, and enjoy.

2 cups superfine blanched almond flour

¼ cup superfine coconut flour

1 teaspoon baking powder

¼ teaspoon salt

8 tablespoons (1 stick) unsalted butter, softened

4 ounces full-fat cream cheese, softened

⅓ cup Swerve granulated sweetener

1 large egg

1 teaspoon almond extract

1. In a small bowl, combine the almond flour, coconut flour, baking powder, and salt. Stir until well combined; set aside.

2. In a large bowl, combine the butter, cream cheese, and sweetener. Beat with an electric mixer on medium until the mixture is fluffy. Add the egg and almond extract and beat until well combined. Slowly add the dry ingredients to the wet ingredients, beating on low. Cover the bowl and chill the dough for 30 minutes.

3. Preheat the oven to 350°F. Line a large rimmed baking sheet with parchment paper.

4. Drop the chilled dough in twelve 2-tablespoon portions onto the prepared pan. Flatten each cookie slightly.

ACTIVE TIME: 20 minutes

TOTAL TIME: 1 hour 15 minutes

SERVINGS: 12 (1 COOKIE EACH)

DIETARY CONSIDERATIONS
Vegetarian

MACROS
84% Fat
5% Carbs
10% Protein

PER SERVING
Calories: 226
Total Fat: 21g
Total Carbs: 11g
Net Carbs: 3g
Fiber: 3g
Sugar: 1g
Protein: 6g

5. Bake for 22 minutes, or until golden brown. Cool the cookies on the pan on a wire rack for 10 minutes. Remove the cookies from the pan and cool completely on the rack.

VARIATIONS

JAM THUMBPRINT COOKIES

Before baking, press the center of each cookie with your thumb to create an indentation. Fill with sugar-free preserves and bake as directed.

CITRUS CREAM CHEESE COOKIES

Substitute orange extract for the almond extract. Add 1 tablespoon grated orange zest with the extract. Or use lemon extract and lemon zest.

CARROT CAKE
page 113

**CHOCOLATE CUPCAKES
WITH CREAM CHEESE
FROSTING**
page 119

ZUCCHINI BREAD
page 88

CARROT CAKE

I get into trouble with readers sometimes when I suggest recipes with the slightest amount of carrot. But you know what? If you want to avoid a bit of carrot in your cake while on keto, you can omit it, or add drained zucchini or whatever else you prefer. But if you're craving carrot cake, you may be willing to enjoy this cake, given that the 1 tablespoon of carrots per serving of this keto cake is less likely to play havoc with your insulin or blood sugar than succumbing to a sugar-laden one.

ACTIVE TIME: 10 minutes

TOTAL TIME: 1 hour

SERVINGS: 8

DIETARY CONSIDERATIONS

Vegetarian

MACROS

86% Fat

4% Carbs

9% Protein

PER SERVING

Calories: 281

Total Fat: 27g

Total Carbs: 14g

Net Carbs: 3g

Fiber: 3g

Sugar: 2g

Protein: 7g

FOR THE CAKE

Keto cooking spray

3 large eggs

1 cup superfine almond flour

⅓ cup Truvía granulated sweetener

1 teaspoon baking powder

1 teaspoon apple pie spice

¼ cup solid coconut oil

½ cup heavy cream

1 cup shredded carrots

½ cup chopped pecans

TO GARNISH (OPTIONAL)

Cream Cheese Frosting (page 196)

¼ cup chopped pecans

1. For the cake: Preheat the oven to 350°F. Grease an 8-inch round cake pan with cooking spray; set aside.

2. In a large bowl, combine the eggs, almond flour, sweetener, baking powder, apple pie spice, coconut oil, and cream. Beat with an electric mixer on medium until the mixture is fluffy. Fold in the carrots and pecans.

3. Pour the batter into the prepared pan. Bake for 30 to 40 minutes, until a knife inserted into the center of the cake comes out clean.

4. Cool the cake in the pan on a wire rack for 20 minutes. Remove the cake from the pan and cool completely on the wire rack. If desired, top with Cream Cheese Frosting and additional pecans before serving.

PEANUT BUTTER CAKE
page 128

BUTTERY ALMOND
POUND CAKE
page 102

CHOCOLATE-CHEESECAKE
BROWNIES
page 117

CHOCOLATE-CHEESECAKE BROWNIES

These brownies need to be well-cooled before you start to devour them, as they can be a little soft and fudgy when hot. Of course, if you want soft and fudgy, don't let me stop you! Make pretty little swirls with a small spatula and serve up your masterpiece.

ACTIVE TIME: 25 minutes

TOTAL TIME: 1 hour 10 minutes

SERVINGS: 8

DIETARY CONSIDERATIONS

Vegetarian

MACROS

82% Fat

3% Carbs

7% Protein

PER SERVING

Calories: 320

Total Fat: 29g

Total Carbs: 21g

Net Carbs: 2g

Fiber: 1g

Sugar: 1g

Protein: 6g

Keto cooking spray

FOR THE BROWNIE BATTER

½ cup sugar-free chocolate chips

8 tablespoons (1 stick) unsalted butter

3 large eggs

¼ cup Swerve granulated sweetener

1 teaspoon vanilla extract

FOR THE CHEESECAKE BATTER

8 ounces full-fat cream cheese, cubed and softened

1 large egg

3 tablespoons Truvía granulated sweetener

1 teaspoon vanilla extract

1. Preheat the oven to 350°F. Grease an 8-inch square baking pan with cooking spray and line the bottom with parchment paper; set aside.

2. For the brownie batter: In a medium microwave-safe bowl, combine the chocolate chips and butter. Microwave on high for 1 minute, stopping and stirring once. Remove from the microwave and stir until all lumps have melted into the mixture (don't continue to microwave the mixture).

3. In a large bowl, combine the eggs, sweetener, and vanilla. Beat with an electric mixer on medium-high until light and frothy. Slowly pour the melted chocolate mixture into the bowl, beating until well blended. Pour the batter into the prepared pan.

continued...

4. For the cheesecake batter: In a medium bowl, combine the cream cheese, egg, sweetener, and vanilla. Beat with an electric mixer on medium-high until light and frothy. Pour the cheesecake batter on top of the brownie batter. Use a rubber scraper or butter knife to swirl the two batters together slightly.

5. Bake for 35 minutes, or until a knife inserted into the center of the brownie comes out clean. (If you see the edges starting to cook faster than the rest of the brownie, cover the top loosely with foil.)

6. Cool in the pan on a wire rack for 10 minutes. Cut into 8 rectangles. Remove from the pan and cool completely on the wire rack.

CHOCOLATE CUPCAKES WITH CREAM CHEESE FROSTING

Moist, dark, rich, toothsome chocolate cupcakes. Too easy to make, and very hard to keep your non-keto friends away from. On a hot day, this can also be made as a cake in an electric pressure cooker—see the recipe on the TwoSleevers blog. But as written, it's the perfect thing to serve six people, without worrying about leftovers that call your name all day long.

ACTIVE TIME: 30 minutes

TOTAL TIME: 1 hour

SERVINGS: 6

DIETARY CONSIDERATIONS

Vegetarian

MACROS

88% Fat

4% Carbs

Protein: 6g

PER SERVING

Calories: 315

Total Fat: 31g

Total Carbs: 18g

Net Carbs: 3g

Fiber: 2g

Sugar: 2g

Protein: 5g

FOR THE CUPCAKES

Keto cooking spray

⅓ cup Swerve granulated sweetener

4 tablespoons (½ stick) unsalted butter, melted

3 large eggs

½ cup heavy cream

1 teaspoon vanilla extract

¼ cup superfine coconut flour

1 teaspoon baking powder

2 tablespoons unsweetened cocoa powder

¼ teaspoon salt

FOR THE FROSTING

4 ounces full-fat cream cheese, softened

4 tablespoons (½ stick) unsalted butter, softened

1 tablespoon Swerve granulated sweetener

1 teaspoon vanilla extract

1. For the cupcakes: Preheat the oven to 350°F. Grease 6 standard muffin cups with cooking spray; set aside.

2. In a large bowl, combine the sweetener and butter and stir until well combined. Add the eggs, cream, and extract. Beat with an electric mixer on medium-high until light and frothy. Add the coconut flour, baking powder, cocoa powder,

continued...

and salt. Beat until well combined and fairly smooth. (Coconut flours vary in absorbency. If the batter is thicker than regular cake batter, add a little heavy cream and beat to combine.) Divide the batter evenly among the cupcake molds.

3. Bake for 20 minutes, or until the tops spring back lightly when touched and a toothpick inserted into the center of a cupcake comes out clean. Cool completely on a wire rack. Remove from the molds.

4. For the frosting: In a medium bowl, combine the cream cheese, butter, sweetener, and vanilla. Beat with an electric mixer on medium until light and fluffy. Frost the cooled cupcakes with the frosting.

COCONUT MACAROONS

These little cookies lend themselves very easily to keto, and provide a satisfying, chewy, sweet little snack. And they're so easy: Once you whip up the egg whites, it takes no time at all to make the macaroons. Bake them a bit longer if you like the coconut on top a little browned and crunchy.

¼ cup superfine blanched almond flour

2 cups unsweetened flaked coconut

1 tablespoon unsalted butter, melted

1 tablespoon vanilla extract

4 large egg whites

¼ cup Swerve granulated sweetener

1. Preheat the oven to 350°F. Line a large rimmed baking sheet with parchment paper; set aside.

2. In a large bowl, combine the almond flour, coconut, butter, and vanilla. Stir until well blended. In a medium bowl, combine the egg whites and sweetener. Beat with an electric mixer until stiff peaks form. Gently fold the egg whites into the flour mixture.

3. Spoon the batter onto the prepared baking sheet in 12 portions. Bake for 15 to 16 minutes, until the tops of the cookies start to brown slightly.

4. Cool the cookies completely on the pan on a wire rack.

ACTIVE TIME: 25 minutes

TOTAL TIME: 40 minutes

SERVINGS: 12
(1 COOKIE EACH)

DIETARY CONSIDERATIONS

Vegetarian

MACROS

76% Fat

10% Carbs

11% Protein

PER SERVING

Calories: 78

Total Fat: 7g

Total Carbs: 7g

Net Carbs: 2g

Fiber: 1g

Sugar: 1g

Protein: 2g

LEMON-RICOTTA CHEESECAKE

If you buy some ricotta for the Lemon–Poppy Seed Muffins (page 76), you may want to make this recipe as well. It has an entirely different taste and texture than the muffins. I initially developed this cheesecake for the Instant Pot and it became very popular, so I adapted the recipe for the oven as well.

ACTIVE TIME: 25 minutes

TOTAL TIME: 1 hour 20 minutes (+ 6 hours chilling)

SERVINGS: 6

DIETARY CONSIDERATIONS

Vegetarian

MACROS

82% Fat

6% Carbs

12% Protein

PER SERVING

Calories: 205

Total Fat: 19g

Total Carbs: 12g

Net Carbs: 3g

Fiber: 0g

Sugar: 2g

Protein: 6g

FOR THE CAKE

Keto cooking spray

8 ounces full-fat cream cheese, softened

¼ cup Truvía granulated sweetener

⅓ cup whole-milk ricotta cheese

Grated zest and juice of 1 lemon

½ teaspoon lemon extract

2 large eggs

FOR THE TOPPING

2 tablespoons full-fat sour cream

1 teaspoon Truvía granulated sweetener

1. For the cake: Preheat the oven to 350°F. Grease a 6-inch springform pan with cooking spray; set aside.

2. In the bowl of a stand mixer fitted with the paddle attachment, combine the cream cheese, sweetener, ricotta, lemon zest and juice, and lemon extract. Beat on medium until the mixture is smooth with no lumps. Taste to ensure the level of sweetness is to your liking. Add the eggs and beat on low just until they are incorporated (overbeating can result in a cracked cake).

3. Transfer the batter to the prepared pan. Bake for 55 minutes, or until the top is mostly set but the center is still slightly soft.

4. For the topping: In a small bowl, combine the sour cream and sweetener. Spread the topping on the warm cake.

5. Refrigerate the cake for 6 to 8 hours, until completely chilled, before serving.

MAPLE-NUT BLONDIES

As I was creating these keto dessert recipes, I kept making chocolate everything, because . . . chocolate. But I understand that not everyone loves chocolate all the time. Actually, that's a lie: I don't understand it, but I've heard tell. In any case, I created these blondies—and now even a die-hard chocolate fan like me sees why blondies are so popular. The maple extract adds flavor without sugar.

ACTIVE TIME: 15 minutes
TOTAL TIME: 50 minutes (+1 hour chilling)
SERVINGS: 8

DIETARY CONSIDERATIONS
Vegetarian

MACROS
85% Fat
5% Carbs
10% Protein

PER SERVING
Calories: 297
Total Fat: 28g
Total Carbs: 19g
Net Carbs: 4g
Fiber: 3g
Sugar: 1g
Protein: 8g

Keto cooking spray

8 tablespoons (1 stick) unsalted butter, melted

½ cup Swerve granulated sweetener

3 large eggs

1 teaspoon maple extract

1 cup superfine blanched almond flour

¼ cup superfine coconut flour

2 teaspoons baking powder

¾ cup chopped walnuts

1. Preheat the oven to 350°F. Line a 9-inch square baking pan with foil, extending the foil by 2 inches over the edges of the pan on all sides. Coat with cooking spray; set aside.

2. In a large bowl, combine the butter and sweetener and whisk until well blended. Add the eggs and maple extract and whisk until well blended. Add the almond flour, coconut flour, and baking powder and stir until well combined. Stir in the walnuts.

3. Pour the batter into the prepared pan. Bake for 35 minutes, or until a toothpick inserted into the center of the blondies comes out clean.

4. Cool in the pan in the refrigerator for 1 hour to firm up. Using the overhanging foil as handles, remove the blondies from the pan. Cut into 8 squares.

PEANUT BUTTER CAKE

I will tell you something that may cause some of you to say, "Eww." I love eating peanut butter off a spoon. Some nights when it's too late to eat but I'm hungry, I eat peanut butter by itself as a little fat bomb. It makes my dog, Gracie, very happy since she gets to share it with me. This peanut butter cake is very peanut-buttery and such a good way to get my favorite flavor into my favorite baked good: cake.

ACTIVE TIME: 15 minutes

TOTAL TIME: 55 minutes

SERVINGS: 8

DIETARY CONSIDERATIONS
Vegetarian

MACROS
75% Fat
5% Carbs
13% Protein

PER SERVING
Calories: 155
Total Fat: 13g
Total Carbs: 16g
Net Carbs: 2g
Fiber: 2g
Sugar: 1g
Protein: 5g

4 tablespoons (½ stick) unsalted butter, plus softened butter for greasing the pan

¼ cup creamy no-sugar-added peanut butter

½ cup Swerve granulated sweetener

3 large eggs

¼ cup superfine coconut flour

2 teaspoons vanilla extract

1½ teaspoons baking powder

1½ teaspoons ground cinnamon, plus additional for dusting

1. Preheat the oven to 350°F. Butter a 7-inch Bundt pan; set aside.

2. In the bowl of a stand mixer fitted with the whisk attachment, combine the butter, peanut butter, and sweetener and whip and aerate the mixture until it is light and soft peaks form, 3 to 4 minutes.

3. Add the eggs, one at a time, beating after each addition before adding the next. Add the coconut flour, vanilla, baking powder, and cinnamon and whisk on low until well blended.

4. Pour the batter into the prepared pan. Bake for 30 minutes, or until a tooth-pick inserted into the center of the cake comes out clean.

5. Cool the cake in the pan on a wire rack for 10 minutes. Remove from the pan and cool completely on the rack. Dust with cinnamon before serving.

SPICE COOKIES

My son Alex makes these again and again—and pretty much eats them all before we can get to them. They're easy to make and just so perfect—not just for the holidays, but anytime. Once again this is a base recipe that can be modified with the spices of your choice.

4 tablespoons (½ stick) unsalted butter, softened, or solid coconut oil

1 large egg

1 tablespoon water

2½ cups superfine blanched almond flour

⅓ cup Truvía granulated sweetener

1 teaspoon baking soda

2 teaspoons ground ginger

1 teaspoon ground cinnamon

½ teaspoon ground nutmeg

¼ teaspoon salt

1. Preheat the oven to 350°F. Line a large rimmed baking sheet with parchment paper; set aside.

2. In a large bowl, combine the butter, egg, and water. Beat with an electric mixer on low until well blended. In a medium bowl, combine the almond flour, sweetener, baking soda, ginger, cinnamon, nutmeg, and salt. Stir until well blended. Add the dry ingredients to the wet ingredients and beat on low until well blended.

3. Roll the dough into eighteen 2-teaspoon-size balls and arrange on the prepared pan, leaving some room between them. Bake for 12 to 15 minutes, until the tops are lightly browned.

4. Cool the cookies on the pan on a wire rack for 5 minutes. Remove from the pan and cool completely on the rack. Store in an airtight container.

ACTIVE TIME: 25 minutes

TOTAL TIME: 45 minutes

SERVINGS: 18 (1 COOKIE EACH)

DIETARY CONSIDERATIONS
Vegetarian

MACROS
82% Fat
3% Carbs
13% Protein

PER SERVING
Calories: 117
Total Fat: 11g
Total Carbs: 7g
Net Carbs: 1g
Fiber: 2g
Sugar: 1g
Protein: 4g

CHOCOLATE
& FAT BOMBS

MILKY BEARS

Do you have to have the little bear molds for this recipe? You do not. Are they cuter and more delicious when made into little bears? I think so! You can use small candy molds of any sort for this, but if you get the little bear molds, I also provide a regular non-milky gummy bear variation on page 136. Note that if you want them chewier, unmold them once they've set and let them rest uncovered in the refrigerator for a few hours.

¼ cup cool water

2 (.25-ounce) packets unflavored powdered gelatin (3 tablespoons)

1 (13.5-ounce) can full-fat coconut milk

3 tablespoons Truvía granulated sweetener

2 or 3 drops pandan extract or other extract

1. Place two 50-cavity silicone gummy bear molds on a large rimmed baking sheet. (If you don't have gummy bear molds, you can use any type of silicone mold for chocolates that totals about 100 cavities.)

2. Pour the water into a small bowl. Sprinkle the gelatin over the water. Set aside to allow the gelatin to soften.

3. Meanwhile, in a small saucepan, combine the coconut milk, sweetener, and pandan extract. Heat over medium-low heat until bubbles start to form around the sides of the pan. Whisk in the softened gelatin. (A flat wire whisk makes this task much easier.)

4. Use the dropper that came with the gummy bear mold to fill the cavities with the gelatin mixture, taking care to fill the ears as well. Refrigerate the filled molds overnight.

continued...

ACTIVE TIME: 30 minutes

TOTAL TIME: 30 minutes (+ overnight chilling)

SERVINGS: 10 (10 BEARS EACH)

DIETARY CONSIDERATIONS

Egg-Free

Dairy-Free

MACROS

77% Fat

6% Carbs

11% Protein

PER SERVING

Calories: 62

Total Fat: 5g

Total Carbs: 5g

Net Carbs: 1g

Fiber: 0g

Sugar: 1g

Protein: 2g

5. Unmold the bears onto the baking sheet. (At this point, if you would like the bears to be chewier, chill, them in the refrigerator uncovered, for an additional 3 to 4 hours.)

6. Store the bears in a tightly sealed container in the refrigerator.

VARIATION

HOMEMADE GUMMY BEARS

In a small saucepan, combine 1 (1.3-ounce) package sugar-free Jell-O, ¼ teaspoon unflavored gelatin, and ¼ cup water (or use ½ cup water for slightly softer gummy bears). Cook over medium heat, stirring, until the Jell-O and gelatin have dissolved completely. Place a 50-cavity silicone gummy bear mold on a large rimmed baking sheet. (Alternatively, use a 24-cup mini-muffin pan to make gummy cups.) Use the dropper that came with the gummy bear mold to fill the cavities with the gelatin mixture, taking care to fill the ears as well. Refrigerate until set, about 1 hour. (At this point, if you want the gummies to be chewier, unmold the bears or cups and place on a plate. Refrigerate, uncovered, for an additional 1 hour.) Store the gummy bears in a tightly sealed container in the refrigerator.

ALMOND BUTTER-CHOCOLATE BOMBS

These three-ingredient fat bombs cook in less than 5 minutes in your microwave. Freeze them overnight and grab one when you're craving some chocolate. Substitute any sort of butter for the almond butter and enjoy endless variations.

½ cup solid coconut oil

¼ cup no-sugar-added almond butter

¼ cup sugar-free chocolate chips

1. Line a mini-muffin pan with paper liners.

2. In a small microwave-safe bowl, combine the coconut oil, almond butter, and chocolate chips. Microwave on high for 1 minute; stir. Microwave in 1-minute increments, stirring after each, until the ingredients are well blended.

3. Divide the mixture evenly among the prepared muffin cups. Freeze until firm, at least 2 hours or up to overnight.

ACTIVE TIME: 10 minutes
TOTAL TIME: 10 minutes
(+ 2 hours freezing)
SERVINGS: 12
(2 BOMBS EACH)

DIETARY CONSIDERATIONS
Egg-Free
Dairy-Free
Vegan

MACROS
88% Fat
3% Carbs
4% Protein

PER SERVING
Calories: 137
Total Fat: 13g
Total Carbs: 4g
Net Carbs: 1g
Fiber: 1g
Sugar: 0g
Protein: 1g

CRANBERRY CHOCOLATE BARK

Many of us won't worry about the 2 tablespoons of cranberries across all those servings, but if they concern you, use unsweetened dried cherries or additional nuts instead. But when the world around you is enjoying cranberries during the holidays and you're feeling left out? This may be how you get over that hurt. Keep the bark refrigerated for the best consistency.

½ cup sugar-free chocolate chips

½ cup solid coconut oil

2 tablespoons unsweetened shredded coconut

2 tablespoons sliced almonds

2 tablespoons dried cranberries or no-sugar-added dried cherries

1. Line a 9-inch pie plate with a circle of parchment paper; set aside.

2. In the top of a double boiler, combine the chocolate chips and coconut oil. Heat until melted and well combined, stirring occasionally.

3. Add the coconut, almonds, and cranberries. Stir well to combine. Pour the mixture into the prepared pie plate. Refrigerate to allow the bark to set until solid.

4. Turn the bark out onto a work surface and break it into bite-size pieces.

ACTIVE TIME: 20 minutes

TOTAL TIME: 20 minutes

SERVINGS: 16

DIETARY CONSIDERATIONS

Egg-Free

Dairy-Free

Vegan

MACROS

82% Fat

4% Carbs

2% Protein

PER SERVING

Calories: 105

Total Fat: 10g

Total Carbs: 6g

Net Carbs: 1g

Fiber: 1g

Sugar: 1g

Protein: 1g

COCONUT FUDGE

NO COOK

This low-carb fudge is a great way to satisfy that sweet tooth without guilt. The chocolate flavor is enough to please any chocolate lover, and the coconut adds great taste and crisp texture. I know it sounds like an odd list of ingredients, but #trustUrvashi and make this easy, chewy, fudgy confection.

ACTIVE TIME: 15 minutes

TOTAL TIME: 15 minutes

SERVINGS: 16

DIETARY CONSIDERATIONS

Egg-Free

Vegetarian

MACROS

70% Fat

12% Carbs

18% Protein

PER SERVING

Calories: 130

Total Fat: 10g

Total Carbs: 8g

Net Carbs: 4g

Fiber: 1g

Sugar: 3g

Protein: 6g

Keto cooking spray

⅓ cup solid coconut oil

¼ cup heavy cream

2 tablespoons sugar-free English toffee–flavored syrup

1 tablespoon unsalted butter

1 cup chocolate whey protein

⅔ cup powdered whole milk

½ cup unsweetened cocoa powder

¼ cup Swerve granulated sweetener

1 cup unsweetened shredded coconut

1. Spray an 8-inch square baking pan with cooking spray; set aside.

2. In a food processor, combine the coconut oil, cream, syrup, butter, whey protein, powdered milk, cocoa powder, and sweetener. Process until smooth. Transfer the mixture to a medium bowl and stir in ¾ cup of the shredded coconut.

3. Press the mixture into the prepared pan. Sprinkle the remaining ¼ cup coconut over the top, pressing lightly with the back of a spoon to help it adhere.

4. Cover the pan with plastic wrap and refrigerate until firm. Cut into 16 squares.

VARIATION

You can also use sugar-free vanilla syrup instead of the English toffee syrup.

MILK CHOCOLATE TRUFFLES

I'm an overachiever. So it's not enough that these have to be delicious keto chocolate truffles—I had to ensure that they were also fat bombs because I'm all about #ruthlessefficiency. They're easy to make and perfect to keep on hand for when you need a little something sweet or a bump in your fat macros.

Keto cooking spray

½ cup sugar-free chocolate chips

1 tablespoon unsalted butter

¼ cup heavy cream

1. Spray a 12-cavity truffle mold (with a capacity of about 1 teaspoon per cavity) with cooking spray; set aside.

2. In a 2-cup heatproof measuring cup with a lip, combine the chocolate chips, butter, and cream. Microwave on high for 30 seconds. Stir well. If the ingredients are not well blended, microwave in 10-second increments, stirring after each one. Do not overcook.

3. Pour the mixture into the truffle molds. Freeze for 30 minutes. Unmold the truffles onto a plate, then chill for 1 hour, or until set.

4. Store the truffles in a tightly covered container in the refrigerator.

ACTIVE TIME: 15 minutes

TOTAL TIME: 45 minutes
(+1 hour chilling)

SERVINGS: 6
(2 TRUFFLES EACH)

DIETARY CONSIDERATIONS
Egg-Free
Vegetarian

MACROS
76% Fat
4% Carbs
2% Protein

PER SERVING
Calories: 184
Total Fat: 16g
Total Carbs: 12g
Net Carbs: 2g
Fiber: 1g
Sugar: 0g
Protein: 1g

MINT CHOCOLATE BARS

These taste a lot like Andes mints. This is another treat that you can easily serve to your friends who don't follow keto and get no complaints. I love the taste and texture contrasts of the firmer chocolate layer and the creamy mint layer.

ACTIVE TIME: 15 minutes

TOTAL TIME: 30 minutes

SERVINGS: 12 (1 BAR EACH)

DIETARY CONSIDERATIONS
Egg-Free
Vegetarian

MACROS
79% Fat
5% Carbs
5% Protein

PER SERVING
Calories: 247
Total Fat: 22g
Total Carbs: 18g
Net Carbs: 3g
Fiber: 2g
Sugar: 1g
Protein: 3g

FOR THE CHOCOLATE BASE

4 tablespoons (½ stick) unsalted butter

1 cup sugar-free chocolate chips

1 cup superfine blanched almond flour

FOR THE MINT TOPPING

4 tablespoons (½ stick) unsalted butter, softened

6 tablespoons heavy cream

1 teaspoon peppermint extract

1 drop green food coloring

⅓ cup Swerve confectioners' sweetener

1. For the base: Line an 8-inch square baking pan with parchment paper. Combine the butter and chocolate chips in a large microwave-safe bowl. Microwave for 15 to 20 seconds on high. Stir until well combined. If the butter and chocolate chips are not completely melted, microwave in 5-second increments, stirring after each.

2. Add the almond flour; stir until well blended. Pat the mixture into the prepared pan and place in the refrigerator.

3. For the topping: In a small bowl, combine the butter, cream, peppermint extract, and food coloring. Beat with an electric mixer on medium until well combined. Gradually add the sweetener, beating on low, until the mixture is smooth.

4. Spread the topping evenly over the base. Refrigerate for 15 to 20 minutes, until firm but not hard. Cut into 12 bars. Store, covered, in the refrigerator.

PEANUT BUTTER BITES

Full confession: I originally put these in the freezer to keep myself from eating all of them in one go. But unfortunately (fortunately?), they taste great frozen as well, so they still don't last very long. I use a small truffle mold and it's just about the right amount for a quick little bite.

½ cup creamy no-sugar-added peanut butter

8 tablespoons (1 stick) unsalted butter

2 tablespoons Swerve confectioners' sweetener

1 teaspoon vanilla extract

1. In a medium microwave-safe bowl, combine the peanut butter, butter, and sweetener. Microwave on high in 30-second increments, stirring after each, until the mixture is completely melted. Add the vanilla and stir until all the sweetener is dissolved.

2. Pour the mixture into a 24-cavity truffle mold. (Alternatively, line the bottom and sides of an 8-inch square baking pan with parchment paper and pour the mixture into the pan.)

3. Freeze for 2 to 4 hours, until set. Unmold the bites. (If using a baking pan, cut into 24 squares.) Transfer the bites to a tightly sealed container or resealable freezer bag. Store in the freezer until ready to eat.

ACTIVE TIME: 15 minutes
TOTAL TIME: 15 minutes
(+ 2 hours freezing)
SERVINGS: 12
(2 BITES EACH)

DIETARY CONSIDERATIONS
Egg-Free
Vegetarian

MACROS
86% Fat
3% Carbs
8% Protein

PER SERVING
Calories: 136
Total Fat: 13g
Total Carbs: 4g
Net Carbs: 1g
Fiber: 1g
Sugar: 0g
Protein: 3g

PEANUT BUTTER-CHOCOLATE BARS

I am a bad mom: I used to steal all the peanut butter cups from my kids' Halloween haul. They both knew better than to eat them without sharing them with me. These bars are the closest you will come to regular peanut butter cups. The recipe is one of the most visited on my blog, and with good reason. You really do need to try them.

¾ cup superfine blanched almond flour

½ cup creamy no-sugar-added peanut butter

4 tablespoons (½ stick) unsalted butter, softened

¼ cup Swerve confectioners' sweetener

½ teaspoon vanilla extract

½ cup sugar-free chocolate chips

1. In a medium bowl, combine the almond flour, peanut butter, butter, sweetener, and vanilla. Stir until well blended. Press into the bottom of a 6-inch square baking pan.

2. Place the chocolate chips in a small microwave-safe bowl. Microwave on high for 30 seconds; stir. If all the chips aren't completely melted, microwave in 10-second increments, stirring after each. Spread the melted chocolate on top of the peanut butter mixture.

3. Chill in the refrigerator for 1 to 2 hours, until firm. Cut into bars.

ACTIVE TIME: 15 minutes
TOTAL TIME: 15 minutes (+1 hour chilling)
SERVINGS: 8 (1 BAR EACH)

DIETARY CONSIDERATIONS
Egg-Free
Vegetarian

MACROS
75% Fat
16% Carbs
10% Protein

PER SERVING
Calories: 282
Total Fat: 24g
Total Carbs: 19g
Net Carbs: 11g
Fiber: 3g
Sugar: 1g
Protein: 7g

SALTED CARAMEL-PECAN PRALINES

When I say *praline,* I'm talking about the Tex-Mex version that you can get at most Tex-Mex restaurants. So sweet it will hurt your teeth, but with caramel-y, nutty goodness. It took me three tries to get this one right. They're still a little more likely to crumble than their sugared cousins, so use a delicate hand when enjoying them; but then again, I'd be surprised if they were around long enough for you to worry about this.

4 tablespoons (½ stick) unsalted butter

¼ cup heavy cream

¼ cup Truvía granulated sweetener

¼ teaspoon salt

¾ cup chopped pecans, toasted

1. Line a rimmed baking sheet with parchment paper; set aside.

2. In a small saucepan, combine the butter, cream, sweetener, and salt. Bring to a boil over medium heat. When it starts to boil, whisk frequently until the mixture is foamy, thick, and light tan in color, about 5 minutes. (If you have a digital thermometer, heat to 280°F to 290°F.)

3. Remove the pan from the heat. Working quickly, add the pecans and stir to coat. Pour the mixture onto the prepared pan and spread it into an even layer about ¼ inch thick.

4. Let stand until completely cool. Break into 8 pieces.

ACTIVE TIME: 15 minutes

TOTAL TIME: 45 minutes

SERVINGS: 8
(1 PRALINE EACH)

DIETARY CONSIDERATIONS
Egg-Free
Vegetarian

MACROS
94% Fat
3% Carbs
3% Protein

PER SERVING
Calories: 149
Total Fat: 16g
Total Carbs: 8g
Net Carbs: 1g
Fiber: 1g
Sugar: 1g
Protein: 1g

RECIPE NOTES

The sweetener will crystallize a little bit in the pralines, but they are still very delicious and quite close to the original version. Chilling will cause the crystals to become more pronounced, so these are best eaten the same day they are made.

SWEET CREAM TRUFFLES

My brother and I used to make these truffles when we got home from school. Of course, as hungry teenagers, we didn't stop to mold them into delicate shapes or even cover with chocolate. We just scarfed down the delicious cream and sugar mixture. Your turn to start scarfing!

2 cups heavy cream

½ cup Swerve confectioners' sweetener

½ cup sugar-free chocolate chips

1 tablespoon unsalted butter

1. Line a rimmed baking sheet with parchment paper; set aside.

2. In a medium saucepan, combine the cream and sweetener. Cook over medium heat, stirring frequently, until the mixture turns light brown and thickens slightly, 5 to 6 minutes. Transfer the mixture to a small bowl and chill until firm, about 1 hour.

3. When the mixture is firm, form it into 12 small balls. Arrange the balls on a plate and chill in the refrigerator while you prepare the coating.

4. In a small microwave-safe bowl, combine the chocolate chips and butter. Microwave on high for 30 seconds; stir. Let stand for 1 minute and stir again to melt any remaining unmelted chocolate or butter.

5. Working quickly, spear each sweet cream ball with a fork and dip into the chocolate coating. (You may find it helpful to put the bowl of chocolate in a pan of hot water to keep it liquid—just don't splash any water into the chocolate or it will seize up!) Place each coated truffle on the prepared pan. Chill in the refrigerator for 1 to 2 hours, until firm.

6. Store the truffles in a tightly sealed container in the refrigerator.

ACTIVE TIME: 30 minutes

TOTAL TIME: 30 minutes (+ 2 hours chilling)

SERVINGS: 6 (2 TRUFFLES EACH)

DIETARY CONSIDERATIONS

Egg-Free

Vegetarian

MACROS

87% Fat

4% Carbs

3% Protein

PER SERVING

Calories: 382

Total Fat: 37g

Total Carbs: 26g

Net Carbs: 4g

Fiber: 1g

Sugar: 2g

Protein: 3g

DRINKS,
ICE CREAM &
ICE POPS

STRAWBERRIES & CREAM ICE CREAM BITES

These are little frozen bites of deliciousness. It's hard to believe you can have strawberry ice cream while on a "diet," but if you've adopted a keto way of living, you know it's not a diet, just a way of eating. I made these in my truffle mold, so as to exercise some semblance of portion control, but you can also freeze it as ice cream. In that case, you may want to double the recipe (see Variations).

½ cup chopped strawberries

⅓ cup Swerve confectioners' sweetener

2 tablespoons water

1 teaspoon lime juice

4 ounces full-fat cream cheese, softened

½ cup heavy cream

1. In large microwave-safe bowl, combine the strawberries, sweetener, and water. Microwave on high, stopping and stirring every 30 seconds for 2 minutes, or until the strawberries are softened.

2. Add the lime juice, cream cheese, and heavy cream. Beat with an electric mixer on high until well combined. Divide the mixture among 24 cavities of a silicone truffle mold. Freeze for 2 to 3 hours, until firm, before serving.

VARIATIONS

STRAWBERRIES & CREAM ICE CREAM

Double the recipe. Transfer the mixture to an ice cream maker and churn for 25 to 30 minutes, until the ice cream is set. At this point, you can serve as a soft-serve ice cream or cure in the freezer for 1 to 2 hours and serve firm. (For this option, let stand at room temperature for 15 minutes before serving.)

continued...

ACTIVE TIME: 25 minutes

TOTAL TIME: 25 minutes
(+ 2 hours freezing)

SERVINGS: 6
(4 BITES EACH)

DIETARY CONSIDERATIONS
Egg-Free
Vegetarian

MACROS
86% Fat
8% Carbs
5% Protein

PER SERVING
Calories: 142
Total Fat: 14g
Total Carbs: 11g
Net Carbs: 3g
Fiber: 0g
Sugar: 2g
Protein: 2g

BLUEBERRIES & CREAM ICE CREAM BITES

Instead of the strawberries and lime juice, use blueberries and lemon juice.

RASPBERRIES & CREAM ICE CREAM BITES

Instead of the strawberries and lime juice, use raspberries and add 1 teaspoon almond extract.

BLUEBERRY ICE CREAM

When I first made this, I had visions of creamy goodness laced with rivers of blueberry deliciousness running through the cream. I got a little too enthusiastic with my spatula as I swirled, and it probably wasn't as pretty as I had intended, but it tasted good—so who cares, right? If done right, though, this makes a very pretty ice cream. This ice cream, like many ice creams that aren't cooked, is best eaten fresh. There's your excuse for eating it all in one day.

ACTIVE TIME: 25 minutes

TOTAL TIME: 40 minutes (+4 hours freezing)

SERVINGS: 8 (½ CUP EACH)

DIETARY CONSIDERATIONS
Egg-Free
Vegetarian

MACROS
84% Fat
9% Carbs
5% Protein

PER SERVING
Calories: 213
Total Fat: 20g
Total Carbs: 12g
Net Carbs: 5g
Fiber: 1g
Sugar: 4g
Protein: 3g

1 cup frozen blueberries, thawed and undrained

¼ cup Truvía granulated sweetener

1 teaspoon xanthan gum

8 ounces full-fat cream cheese, cubed and softened

1 cup full-fat sour cream

½ cup heavy cream

1 teaspoon lemon extract

1. In a medium microwave-safe bowl, combine the blueberries and their juice, the sweetener, and xanthan gum. Microwave on high for 2 minutes, or until the mixture boils and thickens slightly. Refrigerate for 15 to 20 minutes, until completely cooled.

2. In the bowl of a stand mixer fitted with the whisk attachment, combine the cream cheese, sour cream, cream, and lemon extract. Beat on medium-high until the mixture is fluffy. Spoon into a loaf pan. Top with spoonfuls of the

blueberry mixture. Using a spatula, deeply but gently swirl the blueberry mixture into the cream cheese mixture, without combining the two completely.

3. Cover and freeze for 4 to 5 hours, until firm, before serving.

RECIPE NOTE

If left in the freezer for more than 1 day, this ice cream hardens to the point that it becomes somewhat difficult to scoop. If you plan on storing it for more than 1 day, line the loaf pan with parchment paper, leaving an overhang. When you want to serve the ice cream, lift the loaf out of the pan using the overhanging parchment as handles and cut into slices.

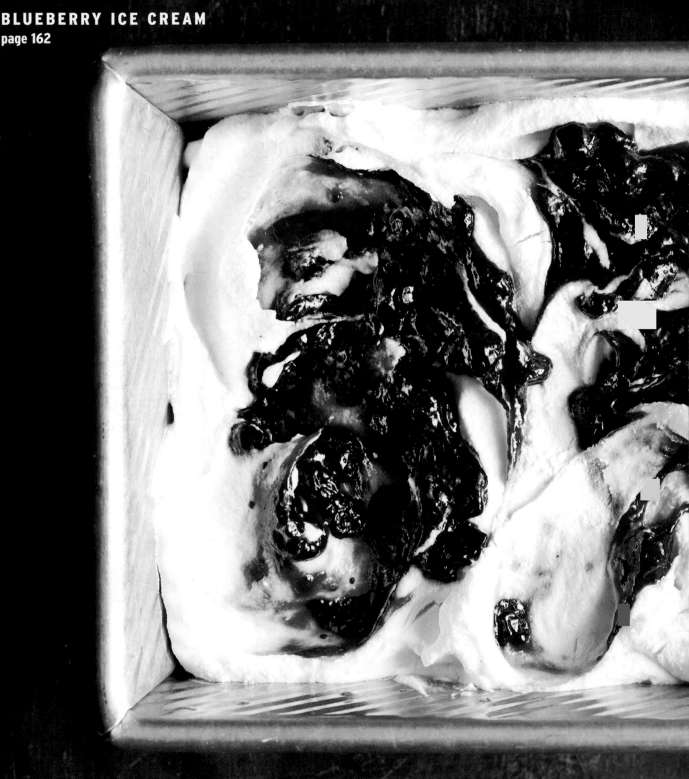

BLUEBERRY ICE CREAM
page 162

BANANA ICE CREAM

NO COOK

Yeah, we can't really have bananas and be keto, can we? Using banana extract is a great way to get a hint of the flavor you may be missing, without the carbs. When I first made this ice cream, I just used vanilla extract—so think of this as a great base recipe for ice cream and get creative with the flavors.

ACTIVE TIME: 20 minutes

TOTAL TIME: 45 minutes

SERVINGS: 8

DIETARY CONSIDERATIONS
Egg-Free
Vegetarian

MACROS
92% Fat
4% Carbs
4% Protein

PER SERVING
Calories: 208
Total Fat: 21g
Total Carbs: 7g
Net Carbs: 2g
Fiber: 0g
Sugar: 2g
Protein: 2g

4 ounces full-fat cream cheese, softened

¼ cup Swerve confectioners' sweetener

1½ cups heavy cream

1 cup unsweetened almond milk

1 teaspoon banana extract

2 or 3 drops yellow food coloring (optional)

1. In a large bowl, combine the cream cheese and sweetener. Beat with an electric mixer on medium until well blended. Gradually add the heavy cream, beating constantly. Beat on medium-high until the mixture is light and fluffy and firm peaks form.

2. Add the almond milk, banana extract, and food coloring (if using). Stir gently until blended.

3. Transfer the mixture to an ice cream maker and churn for 25 to 30 minutes, until the ice cream is set. At this point, you can serve it as a soft-serve ice cream or cure it in the freezer for 1 to 2 hours to serve firm. (For this option, let it stand at room temperature for 15 minutes before serving.)

VARIATIONS

COCONUT ICE CREAM

Omit the banana extract and food coloring. Add ½ teaspoon coconut extract and ½ cup toasted unsweetened shredded coconut.

FRUIT ICE CREAM

Omit the banana extract and food coloring. Reduce the almond milk to ½ cup. Add ½ to ¾ cup pure fruit puree. (Be sure to use lower-carb fruits, such as berries.)

ICE CREAM BITES

Cut the recipe in half and use a silicone truffle mold or silicone cupcake molds to freeze the mixture in small bite-size chunks.

AVOCADO-LIME ICE POPS

Lime elevates ice pops to something unexpected and surprisingly sophisticated. Using coconut milk allows you to enjoy a vegan ice pop that is a fat bomb, and also very creamy.

1 large ripe avocado (about 1 cup flesh)

1 (14.5-ounce) can full-fat coconut milk

¼ cup Swerve granulated sweetener

1 tablespoon lime juice

1. In a blender, combine the avocado, coconut milk, sweetener, and lime juice. Blend until smooth (the mixture will be quite thick).

2. Divide among six ice pop molds. Freeze until firm, 4 to 6 hours.

ACTIVE TIME: 10 minutes
TOTAL TIME: 10 minutes
(+ 4 hours freezing)
SERVINGS: 6

DIETARY CONSIDERATIONS
Egg-Free
Dairy-Free
Vegan

MACROS
82% Fat
5% Carbs
4% Protein

PER SERVING
Calories: 167
Total Fat: 15g
Total Carbs: 13g
Net Carbs: 2g
Fiber: 3g
Sugar: 2g
Protein: 2g

CANTALOUPE ICE POPS

Summertime, with all of its fresh fruits, can be hard if you're on a strict keto diet. But I've found that I don't really need to eat a whole cantaloupe just to feel like I've partaken of summer's bounty. A taste or two fulfills me. These cantaloupe pops use very little cantaloupe across several pops. It's one of the ways to enjoy the taste of the fruit without going overboard.

1½ cups chopped ripe cantaloupe

1 cup unsweetened almond milk

½ cup heavy cream

4 ounces mascarpone cheese

¼ cup Truvía granulated sweetener

¼ cup lime juice

2 tablespoons powdered whole milk

1 teaspoon xanthan gum

1. In a blender, combine the cantaloupe, almond milk, cream, mascarpone, sweetener, lime juice, powdered milk, and xanthan gum. Blend on medium-high until very smooth.

2. Divide among ten ice pop molds. Freeze for 4 to 6 hours, until solid. (Alternatively, churn in an ice cream maker until set. The mixture will still be fairly soft. Transfer to a freezer-safe container. Cover and freeze for an additional 30 minutes.)

ACTIVE TIME: 15 minutes

TOTAL TIME: 15 minutes (+ 4 hours freezing)

SERVINGS: 10

DIETARY CONSIDERATIONS

Egg-Free

Vegetarian

MACROS

83% Fat

11% Carbs

7% Protein

PER SERVING

Calories: 112

Total Fat: 10g

Total Carbs: 9g

Net Carbs: 3g

Fiber: 1g

Sugar: 3g

Protein: 2g

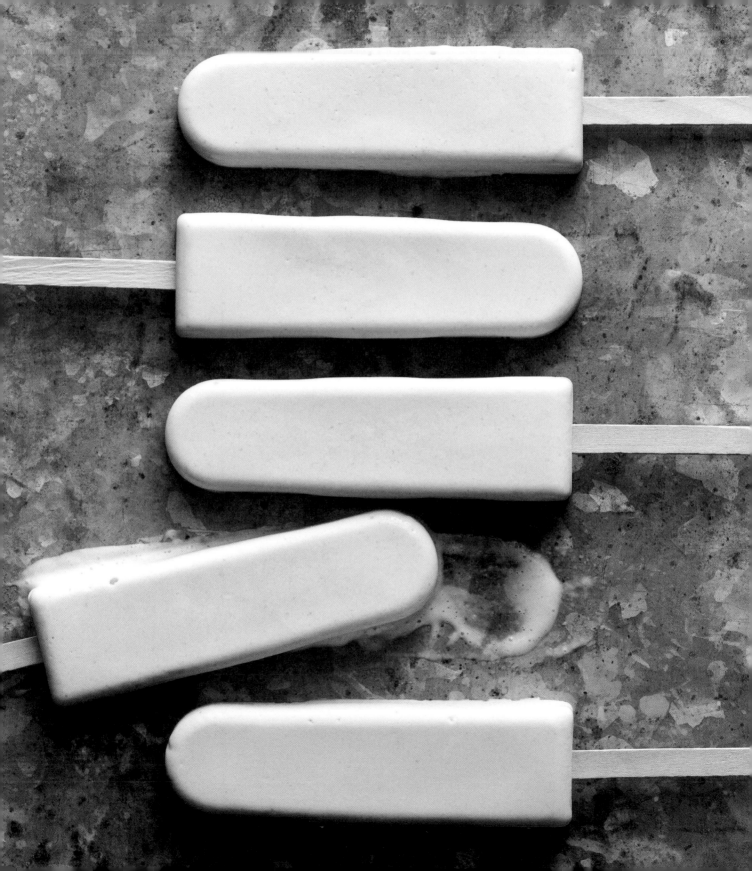

CHOCOLATE FUDGE ICE POPS

Opinions among the taste testers were divided on whether you could taste the avocado in these, and whether that was a good thing. I could taste a hint of avocado, and I thought that was a good thing. Try it for yourself and enjoy the unexpected fudgy goodness of these fat bomb pops.

1 large ripe avocado (1½ to 2 cups flesh)

2½ cups unsweetened almond milk

¼ to ⅓ cup Truvía granulated sweetener

2 tablespoons unsweetened cocoa powder

1. In a blender, combine the avocado, almond milk, sweetener, and cocoa powder. Blend on medium-high until very smooth.

2. Divide among twelve ice pop molds. Freeze for 4 to 6 hours, until solid. (Alternatively, churn in an ice cream maker and serve when set.)

ACTIVE TIME: 10 minutes

TOTAL TIME: 10 minutes
(+ 4 hours freezing)

SERVINGS: 12

DIETARY CONSIDERATIONS

Egg-Free

Dairy-Free

Vegan

MACROS

82% Fat

7% Carbs

6% Protein

PER SERVING

Calories: 56

Total Fat: 5g

Total Carbs: 7g

Net Carbs: 1g

Fiber: 2g

Sugar: 0g

Protein: 1g

COCONUT-PANDAN
ICE POPS

Me and pandan: best buds. But coconut milk and pandan? Clearly meant to be BFFs. They are *so* good together. I will exhort you to get pandan extract, but if not, any of your favorite extracts will do. I've also used just plain ground cinnamon in these and they're absolutely fantastic little frozen fat bombs.

1 (14.5-ounce) can full-fat coconut milk

¼ cup Truvía granulated sweetener

3 or 4 drops pandan extract

1. In a blender, combine the coconut milk, sweetener, and extract. Blend on medium-high until very smooth.

2. Divide among six ice pop molds. Freeze for 4 to 6 hours, until firm. (Alternatively, churn in an ice cream maker and serve when set.)

ACTIVE TIME: 10 minutes

TOTAL TIME: 10 minutes
(+ 4 hours freezing)

SERVINGS: 6

DIETARY CONSIDERATIONS
Egg-Free
Dairy-Free
Vegan

MACROS
82% Fat
8% Carbs
3% Protein

PER SERVING
Calories: 103
Total Fat: 9g
Total Carbs: 10g
Net Carbs: 2g
Fiber: 0g
Sugar: 2g
Protein: 1g

ORANGE CREAM ICE POPS

These have an interesting texture—a little creamy, a little crunchy. I found that texture to be a nice change from the other pops in this book, which are smoother, so I've included the recipe for you to try.

½ cup boiling water

1 (1.3-ounce) package sugar-free orange gelatin

1 cup heavy cream

1. Pour the boiling water into a medium heat-safe bowl. Sprinkle the gelatin on top and let stand for 10 minutes. Stir until the gelatin is well incorporated. (If it's still grainy, microwave on high for 30 seconds and stir again.)

2. Pour the cream into a blender. Add the gelatin mixture. Blend on medium-high until the mixture is creamy and well blended, stopping occasionally to scrape the sides of the jar. (Take care not to overblend and turn the cream into butter—about 30 seconds in a high-powered blender is all you need.)

3. Divide among six ice pop molds. Freeze for 4 to 6 hours, until solid. (Alternatively, churn in an ice cream maker and serve when set.)

RECIPE NOTE

For a vegetarian version, use a vegetarian/agar-agar–based gelatin.

ACTIVE TIME: 25 minutes
TOTAL TIME: 25 minutes
(+ 4 hours freezing)
SERVINGS: 6

DIETARY CONSIDERATIONS
Egg-Free

MACROS
91% Fat
3% Carbs
5% Protein

PER SERVING
Calories: 142
Total Fat: 14g
Total Carbs: 1g
Net Carbs: 1g
Fiber: 0g
Sugar: 1g
Protein: 2g

NUTMEG COFFEE POPS

Who says you have to drink your Bulletproof coffee? Make coffee pops instead and enjoy one whenever you want. I was so in love with these that I had them late one night—and stayed up until 2 a.m. Try not to do that. Oh, and that nutmeg? Classic coffee combination in South India. You'll see why.

1 (13.5-ounce) can full-fat coconut milk

1 cup unsweetened almond milk

⅓ cup Swerve confectioners' sweetener

1 tablespoon espresso powder

⅛ to ¼ teaspoon ground nutmeg

1. In a medium bowl, combine the coconut milk, almond milk, sweetener, espresso powder, and nutmeg to taste. Whisk until well combined.

2. Divide among eight ice pop molds. Freeze for 4 to 6 hours, until solid.

VARIATIONS

MOCHA POPS

Omit the nutmeg. Add 1 tablespoon unsweetened cocoa powder.

CARDAMOM POPS

Omit the nutmeg. Add ½ teaspoon ground cardamom.

BOOZY POPS

Omit the nutmeg. Add 1 to 2 tablespoon Baileys Irish Cream. Note that this will increase the carb count. Do not overdo the alcohol, as it will affect the consistency of the ice pops.

ACTIVE TIME: 10 minutes

TOTAL TIME: 10 minutes (+ 4 hours freezing)

SERVINGS: 8

DIETARY CONSIDERATIONS
Egg-Free
Dairy-Free
Vegan

MACROS
80% Fat
10% Carbs
4% Protein

PER SERVING
Calories: 78
Total Fat: 7g
Total Carbs: 8g
Net Carbs: 2g
Fiber: 0g
Sugar: 1g
Protein: 1g

NO-COOK ICE CREAM

NO COOK

The problem with ice cream that requires you to make a custard base is that it assumes you plan things ahead of time, and that you have the patience to make a custard, cool the custard, then freeze the ice cream—yeah, that's not me. I want ice cream. Now. This recipe lets me have it at virtually a moment's notice. I typically start the machine as we sit down to dinner, and when we're done eating and the table is cleared, our ice cream is ready. Hard to beat that.

ACTIVE TIME: 15 minutes

TOTAL TIME: 40 minutes

SERVINGS: 6

DIETARY CONSIDERATIONS
Egg-Free
Vegetarian

MACROS
88% Fat
6% Carbs
6% Protein

PER SERVING
Calories: 312
Total Fat: 31g
Total Carbs: 16g
Net Carbs: 5g
Fiber: 0g
Sugar: 6g
Protein: 4g

⅓ cup Truvía granulated sweetener

2 tablespoons powdered whole milk

¼ teaspoon xanthan gum

1 cup whole milk

2 cups heavy cream

1 to 2 teaspoons vanilla extract

1. In a large bowl, combine the sweetener, powdered milk, and xanthan gum. Whisk well until there are no lumps. Add the whole milk, cream, and vanilla to taste. Whisk until the sweetener is completely dissolved.

2. Transfer the mixture to an ice cream maker and churn for 25 to 30 minutes, until the ice cream is set. At this point, you can serve it as a soft-serve ice cream, or cure it in the freezer for 1 to 2 hours to serve firm. (For this option, let it stand at room temperature for 15 minutes before serving.)

RECIPE NOTE

This tastes a lot creamier when it's fresh, but a lot more like ice cream when it's been allowed to cure in the freezer. Try it both ways and see which you prefer.

SPICY MEXICAN HOT CHOCOLATE MIX

What is nicer that a cup of hot chocolate on a cold day? A keto version of it that actually tastes good, that's what. I added some cinnamon to mine to mimic the traditional Mexican hot chocolate I love. I usually make a batch of the mix, put it in an airtight tin, and store it for a month or more in the pantry.

1 cup powdered whole milk

½ cup Truvía granulated sweetener

½ cup unsweetened cocoa powder

1 teaspoon xanthan gum

1 tablespoon ground cinnamon

1 teaspoon ancho chile powder, or more to taste

1. In a medium bowl, combine the powdered milk, sweetener, cocoa powder, cornstarch, cinnamon, and chile powder. Whisk until well combined. Store in a tightly sealed container in a cool, dark place until ready to use.

2. To serve, place 2 to 3 tablespoons of the mix in a microwave-safe cup. Add hot water, stirring to blend. Microwave on high for 30 seconds. Stir to blend. (Alternatively, use cool tap water and microwave on high for 1 to 2 minutes, stirring every 30 seconds.)

ACTIVE TIME: 10 minutes

TOTAL TIME: 10 minutes

SERVINGS: 8

DIETARY CONSIDERATIONS

Egg-Free

Vegetarian

MACROS

48% Fat

29% Carbs

19% Protein

PER SERVING

Calories: 96

Total Fat: 5g

Total Carbs: 22g

Net Carbs: 7g

Fiber: 3g

Sugar: 0g

Protein: 5g

ULTRA-RICH MEXICAN SIPPING CHOCOLATE

There's a difference between sipping chocolate and drinking chocolate. The latter can be guzzled, but the former should be served in little demitasse cups and savored. This version is so rich, you will be satisfied with very little.

1 cup unsweetened almond milk

1 cup heavy cream

3 tablespoons Truvía granulated sweetener

3 ounces unsweetened chocolate squares

1 teaspoon ground cinnamon

Pinch of cayenne pepper

1 teaspoon vanilla extract

1. In a medium saucepan, combine the almond milk, cream, sweetener, and chocolate. Heat on medium-low, stirring frequently (do not allow the mixture to come to a rolling boil), until the chocolate is melted and the mixture is heated through. Remove from the heat. Stir in the cinnamon, cayenne, and vanilla.

2. Divide among four demitasse cups and serve.

ACTIVE TIME: 15 minutes

TOTAL TIME: 15 minutes

SERVINGS: 4

DIETARY CONSIDERATIONS

Egg-Free

Vegetarian

MACROS

85% Fat

6% Carbs

6% Protein

PER SERVING

Calories: 353

Total Fat: 33g

Total Carbs: 18g

Net Carbs: 5g

Fiber: 4g

Sugar: 2g

Protein: 5g

VARIATIONS

PEPPERMINT SIPPING CHOCOLATE

Omit the cinnamon and cayenne and substitute peppermint extract for the vanilla.

CHOCOLATE-ORANGE SIPPING CHOCOLATE

Omit the cinnamon and cayenne and substitute orange extract for the vanilla.

DRINKING CHOCOLATE

Mix 1 to 2 tablespoons of the sipping chocolate with 1 cup hot unsweetened almond milk. (You can store the sipping chocolate in the refrigerator for up to 1 week.)

CHOCOLATE GANACHE

My love affair with chocolate continues with this unabashedly rich and chocolaty frosting. There's something so decadent about sticking your finger into frosting and eating it straight from the bowl! We all have memories of stealing a spoonful of frosting while helping Mom cook, so you get a dose of nostalgia and deliciousness in one when you make this.

¾ cup heavy cream

1 tablespoon unsalted butter

1 cup sugar-free chocolate chips

1. Combine the cream and butter in a medium microwave-safe bowl. Microwave on high until very hot, 1 to 2 minutes. Add the chocolate chips. Let stand, stirring occasionally, until the chocolate has melted and the mixture is smooth.

2. *For Chocolate Ganache Glaze:* Use immediately as a pourable glaze.

   For Chocolate Ganache Frosting: Allow the mixture to cool for 20 to 30 minutes. Beat with an electric mixer on medium-high until light and fluffy.

RECIPE NOTE

Leftover ganache may be stored in the refrigerator, covered, for 1 week. Reheat at a low temperature to make it spreadable or pourable.

ACTIVE TIME: 10 minutes

TOTAL TIME: 35 minutes

SERVINGS: 24

DIETARY CONSIDERATIONS

Egg-Free

Vegetarian

MACROS

73% Fat

0% Carbs

3% Protein

PER SERVING

Calories: 76

Total Fat: 6g

Total Carbs: 6g

Net Carbs: 0g

Fiber: 1g

Sugar: 0g

Protein: 1g

continued...

CARDAMOM CUSTARD

I am a huge custard fan. Boiled, steamed, baked—any which way, custard is my friend. It's fairly easy to make it keto-friendly, and it's the ultimate comfort food for many of us. Cardamom-scented custard is an easy win when you're looking for something familiar-but-different.

1 cup heavy cream

1 cup unsweetened almond milk

2 large eggs

⅓ cup Truvía granulated sweetener

½ teaspoon vanilla bean paste or vanilla extract

½ teaspoon ground cardamom, plus additional for garnish

1. Preheat the oven to 350°F.

2. In a medium bowl, combine the cream, almond milk, eggs, sweetener, vanilla, and cardamom. Whisk until well combined.

3. Bring a tea kettle of water to a boil. Arrange four 4-ounce ramekins in a 9-inch square baking pan. Divide the custard mixture among the ramekins. Sprinkle lightly with additional cardamom. Gently place the pan in the oven. Pour hot water from the tea kettle into the baking pan until it reaches halfway up the sides of the ramekins. (Take care not to splash water into the custards.)

4. Bake the custards for 60 to 75 minutes, until set. Monitor the water level during baking to be sure it doesn't all evaporate. If it gets low, add hot tap water using the tea kettle or a glass measuring cup with a pouring spout.

5. Cool the custards on a wire rack for 5 to 10 minutes. Serve warm or cover and chill in the refrigerator until cold before serving.

ACTIVE TIME: 10 minutes

TOTAL TIME: 1 hour 15 minutes

SERVINGS: 4

DIETARY CONSIDERATIONS

Vegetarian

MACROS

89% Fat

3% Carbs

8% Protein

PER SERVING

Calories: 250

Total Fat: 25g

Total Carbs: 18g

Net Carbs: 2g

Fiber: 0g

Sugar: 2g

Protein: 5g

ALMOND PHIRNI

Kheer is a traditional Indian dessert made with either rice or thin noodles (hello, carbs!). I really miss its creamy richness. *Phirni* is a cousin of *kheer*, typically made not with rice, but rather with rice flour (hello again, carbs!). When I decided to try making *phirni* with almond flour I had no idea what to expect. But it was a huge hit with taste testers, and is now an easy go-to for me.

¾ cup heavy cream

1 cup unsweetened almond milk

½ cup superfine blanched almond flour

2 tablespoons Truvía granulated sweetener

½ to 1 teaspoon ground cardamom, plus additional for garnish

2 or 3 saffron threads, crushed

1. In a medium saucepan, combine the cream, almond milk, almond flour, sweetener, cardamom to taste, and saffron. Whisk until well combined. Bring to a boil over medium-high heat. Reduce the heat and simmer, whisking frequently to prevent lumps from forming, until the mixture has the consistency of thin pancake batter, about 5 minutes.

2. Refrigerate until chilled, 1 to 2 hours.

3. Sprinkle with cardamom and serve.

ACTIVE TIME: 25 minutes

TOTAL TIME: 25 minutes (+1 hour chilling)

SERVINGS: 8

DIETARY CONSIDERATIONS

Egg-Free

Vegetarian

MACROS

89% Fat

3% Carbs

8% Protein

PER SERVING

Calories: 121

Total Fat: 12g

Total Carbs: 5g

Net Carbs: 1g

Fiber: 1g

Sugar: 1g

Protein: 2g

COCONUT-PANDAN CHIA SEED PUDDING

Super high in fiber, great tasting, and stupid simple to make. The one thing that really helps chia seed pudding set up quickly is patience for the 10 to 15 minutes it takes for the chia seeds to absorb all or most of the hot water. Waiting a few minutes will pay dividends in the end. If you don't have pandan extract—well, just get some online or in an Asian grocery store. You will thank me. Or use vanilla or almond extract, if you must.

½ cup chia seeds

1½ cups hot water

1 (13.5-ounce) can full-fat coconut milk

½ teaspoon pandan extract

⅓ cup Truvía granulated sweetener

In a medium bowl, combine the chia seeds and hot water. Let stand until all of the water has been absorbed, 10 to 15 minutes. Add the coconut milk, pandan extract, and sweetener. Stir well to combine. Cover and chill in the refrigerator until set, 3 to 4 hours.

ACTIVE TIME: 10 minutes

TOTAL TIME: 15 minutes (+3 hours chilling)

SERVINGS: 6

DIETARY CONSIDERATIONS

Egg-Free

Dairy-Free

Vegan

MACROS

75% Fat

2% Carbs

11% Protein

PER SERVING

Calories: 177

Total Fat: 15g

Total Carbs: 19g

Net Carbs: 1g

Fiber: 7g

Sugar: 2g

Protein: 5g

COCONUT PANNA COTTA

Easy, foolproof, dairy-free panna cotta is a fat bomb that's also very smooth and light tasting. It sets up easily and will continue to get firmer over 6 to 8 hours in the fridge. Or so I'm told. We had one portion that stayed around that long—the rest were devoured a lot sooner.

½ cup cold water

1 (13.5-ounce) can full-fat coconut milk

2 tablespoons Truvía granulated sweetener

¼ teaspoon unflavored powdered gelatin

1 teaspoon vanilla or coconut extract

1. In a medium saucepan, combine the water, coconut milk, and sweetener. Whisk until well combined. Slowly add the gelatin, whisking continuously. (You may see a few small lumps but they will disappear when the mixture is heated.) Cook over medium heat, whisking frequently, until the gelatin and sweetener have completely dissolved. Remove from the heat and whisk in the vanilla.

2. Divide the mixture among six 4-ounce ramekins. Let cool completely. Cover and chill in the refrigerator for 4 to 6 hours, until firm.

ACTIVE TIME: 20 minutes

TOTAL TIME: 20 minutes (+ 4 hours chilling)

SERVINGS: 6

DIETARY CONSIDERATIONS

Egg-Free

Dairy-Free

MACROS

81% Fat

8% Carbs

4% Protein

PER SERVING

Calories: 98

Total Fat: 9g

Total Carbs: 6g

Net Carbs: 2g

Fiber: 0g

Sugar: 2g

Protein: 1g

LEMON MOUSSE

Lemon desserts are wonderful in the summer; in the winter, I think they remind us of the lighter, warmer seasons that await. So I guess what I'm saying is, there's never really a wrong time for a good, easy lemon mousse. This little fat bomb will keep in the fridge for up to a week, so you can make it, then eat little spoonfuls whenever the urge strikes.

8 ounces mascarpone cheese, softened

1 cup heavy cream

½ cup lemon juice

⅓ cup Truvía granulated sweetener

1 teaspoon lemon extract

¼ teaspoon salt

1. In the bowl of a stand mixer fitted with the paddle attachment, combine the mascarpone, cream, lemon juice, sweetener, lemon extract, and salt. Beat on medium until the mixture is smooth and creamy.

2. Divide among four small dessert dishes or ramekins. Cover and chill in the refrigerator until set, 1 to 2 hours.

ACTIVE TIME: 15 minutes

TOTAL TIME: 15 minutes
(+1 hour chilling)

SERVINGS: 4

DIETARY CONSIDERATIONS

Egg-Free

Vegetarian

MACROS

91% Fat

5% Carbs

4% Protein

PER SERVING

Calories: 466

Total Fat: 48g

Total Carbs: 22g

Net Carbs: 6g

Fiber: 0g

Sugar: 3g

Protein: 6g

FRENCH SILK PUDDING

This pudding is like the filling in a classic French silk pie. If you wanted, you could definitely use it to fill the Vegan Pie Crust (page 237), but you really don't have to. It's perfectly spoonable, and lovely served just as a mousse-like pudding.

1 cup heavy cream

2 large eggs, lightly beaten

¾ cup Truvía granulated sweetener

4 ounces unsweetened chocolate squares, chopped

4 tablespoons (½ stick) unsalted butter

1. In a large bowl, beat the cream with an electric mixer until stiff peaks form. Place the whipped cream in the refrigerator.

2. In a small saucepan, whisk the eggs and sweetener until well blended. Add the chocolate and butter. Cook over medium heat, whisking frequently, until the chocolate and butter are melted. Continue to cook, whisking frequently, until the mixture coats the back of a spoon, 5 minutes. Remove from the heat and allow to cool slightly, about 5 minutes.

3. Using a rubber spatula, slowly fold the chocolate mixture into the whipped cream, stirring gently until it is well blended.

4. Divide the mixture among six 4-ounce ramekins. Cover and chill in the refrigerator until set, 1 to 2 hours.

ACTIVE TIME: 30 minutes

TOTAL TIME: 1 hour 30 minutes

SERVINGS: 6

DIETARY CONSIDERATIONS
Vegetarian

MACROS
87% Fat
5% Carbs
7% Protein

PER SERVING
Calories: 349
Total Fat: 34g
Total Carbs: 31g
Net Carbs: 4g
Fiber: 3g
Sugar: 1g
Protein: 6g

HIGH-PROTEIN CHOCOLATE MOUSSE

I first made this recipe almost five years ago, when I started eating keto, and it continues to be a favorite. If you're already over your protein allowance for the day, you might want to reduce the amount of protein powder a little.

2 ounces bittersweet chocolate, chopped

½ cup heavy cream

1½ scoops unflavored protein powder

1. Place the chocolate in a medium microwave-safe bowl. Microwave on high for 1 minute; stir. Continue to microwave in 15- to 20-second increments, stirring after each, until the chocolate is melted. Let cool slightly.

2. In another medium bowl, beat the cream with an electric mixer on medium until soft peaks form. Add the protein powder and beat until medium peaks form. Gently fold in the melted chocolate.

3. Divide among four small dessert dishes or ramekins. Cover and chill in the refrigerator until set, 1 to 2 hours.

ACTIVE TIME: 20 minutes
TOTAL TIME: 20 minutes (+1 hour chilling)
SERVINGS: 4

DIETARY CONSIDERATIONS
Egg-Free
Vegetarian

MACROS
69% Fat
11% Carbs
20% Protein

PER SERVING
Calories: 216
Total Fat: 17g
Total Carbs: 7g
Net Carbs: 6g
Fiber: 1g
Sugar: 5g
Protein: 12g

HIGH-PROTEIN JELL-O MOUSSE

NO COOK

What I like about this recipe is that it's extremely versatile. You can change the flavor of the Jell-O and have a completely different dessert each day. I use Greek yogurt for its slightly lower carb count compared to regular yogurt, but if you really wanted to cut carbs further, you could always make your own "yogurt" out of heavy cream, and use that instead.

1 (0.3-ounce) box sugar-free black cherry Jell-O

½ cup hot water

1¼ cups plain Greek yogurt

2 scoops unflavored protein powder

1. Place the Jell-O in a medium bowl. Pour the hot water over the Jell-O and let stand for 5 minutes.

2. Add the yogurt and protein powder. Beat with an electric mixer on medium until well blended and smooth.

3. Divide among four 4-ounce ramekins. Chill in the refrigerator until set, 2 to 3 hours.

ACTIVE TIME: 10 minutes

TOTAL TIME: 10 minutes (+ 2 hours chilling)

SERVINGS: 4

DIETARY CONSIDERATIONS
Egg-Free

MACROS
18% Fat
11% Carbs
67% Protein

PER SERVING
Calories: 142
Total Fat: 3g
Total Carbs: 4g
Net Carbs: 4g
Fiber: 0g
Sugar: 2g
Protein: 24g

KEY LIME CHEESECAKE

A classic no-bake cheesecake recipe made keto, with little fuss and very few ingredients. You could put this into the Vegan Pie Crust (page 237), or just chill it in a pan and serve crustless slices.

ACTIVE TIME: 10 minutes

TOTAL TIME: 10 minutes (+ 2 hours chilling)

SERVINGS: 4

DIETARY CONSIDERATIONS
Egg-Free

MACROS
85% Fat
6% Carbs
8% Protein

PER SERVING
Calories: 207
Total Fat: 20g
Total Carbs: 3g
Net Carbs: 3g
Fiber: 0g
Sugar: 2g
Protein: 4g

1 (0.3-ounce) package sugar-free lime Jell-O

1 cup boiling water

8 ounces full-fat cream cheese, softened

Thin strips of lime zest, for garnish

1. In a small bowl, combine the gelatin and water. Stir until the gelatin has completely dissolved. (You may need to reheat the mixture in the microwave in 10-second increments to help the gelatin dissolve.)

2. In a medium bowl, beat the cream cheese with an electric mixer until fluffy. Slowly pour in the gelatin mixture and whip until the ingredients are well blended.

3. Divide among four small ramekins. Cover and chill in the refrigerator for 2 to 3 hours, until firm. Garnish with lime zest before serving.

MIXED BERRY CRUMBLE

Adding xanthan gum to berries helps to thicken them, keeping you from using cornstarch, which would be typical in a crumble. This crumble is very good hot, especially when combined with No-Cook Ice Cream (page 178).

ACTIVE TIME: 10 minutes

TOTAL TIME: 30 minutes

SERVINGS: 4

DIETARY CONSIDERATIONS

Grain-Free

Gluten-Free

Egg-Free

Soy-Free

Low-Carb

MACROS

72% Fat

14% Carbs

8% Protein

PER SERVING

Calories: 167

Total Fat: 13g

Total Carbs: 23g

Net Carbs: 6g

Fiber: 5g

Sugar: 5g

Protein: 4g

FOR THE BERRIES

2 cups fresh or frozen mixed berries, thawed

2 tablespoons Truvia granulated sweetener

½ teaspoon xanthan gum

1 tablespoon lemon juice

FOR SERVING

Whipped cream or No-Cook Ice Cream (page 178)

FOR THE TOPPING

¼ cup superfine bleached almond flour

¼ cup thinly sliced almonds

2 tablespoons Truvia granulated sweetener

2 tablespoons unsweetened shredded coconut

2 tablespoons butter or coconut oil, melted

1. Preheat the oven to 350°F.

2. For the berries: In an 8-inch square baking pan, combine the berries, sweetener, xanthan gum, and lemon juice. Toss to combine.

3. For the topping: In a small bowl, combine the flour, almonds, sweetener, coconut, and melted butter.

4. Sprinkle the topping over the berries, covering most of the surface. Bake for 15 minutes or until the berries are cooked and the top has browned. Let cool for 5 minutes before serving. Serve with whipped cream or ice cream.

MIXED BERRY JAM

I've tried buying sugar-free preserves, but they just lack a certain something for me. This homemade jam is a lot more substantial and is actually perfect on Nut & Seed Bread (page 79), Buttery Almond Pound Cake (page 102), or even No-Cook Ice Cream (page 178).

1 cup fresh or thawed frozen mixed berries

1 tablespoon Truvía granulated sweetener

1 tablespoon water

1 tablespoon chia seeds

2 teaspoons lemon juice

1. In a medium saucepan, combine the berries, sweetener, water, and chia seeds. Crush the berries with the back of a spoon to create a rough puree. Cook over medium heat, stirring frequently, until the mixture has thickened, 8 to 10 minutes.

2. Remove from the heat and stir in the lemon juice. Store in a tightly sealed container in the refrigerator for up to 2 weeks.

> ## RECIPE NOTES
>
> *Substitute any single type of berry for the mixed berries.*
>
> *Thin the jam with a little bit of water and serve as a compote with Coconut Panna Cotta (page 210).*
>
> *Do not use pure erythritol in this recipe, as it tends to get grainy when refrigerated.*

ACTIVE TIME: 25 minutes

TOTAL TIME: 25 minutes

SERVINGS: 24 (1 TABLESPOON EACH)

DIETARY CONSIDERATIONS
Egg-Free
Dairy-Free
Vegan

MACROS
36% Fat
0% Carbs
0% Protein

PER SERVING
Calories: 5
Total Fat: 0g
Total Carbs: 1g
Net Carbs: 0g
Fiber: 1g
Sugar: 0g
Protein: 0g

MIXED BERRY CUSTARD

You could serve this either hot or cold; it will be delicious either way. If I were you, I'd make two batches so you can try one hot and the other cold, just to be sure! The custard can also be steamed in a pressure cooker for 20 minutes.

Keto cooking spray

2 cups mixed fresh berries

2 large eggs

¼ cup Swerve granulated sweetener

½ cup superfine blanched almond flour

¼ cup heavy cream

Grated zest and juice of 1 lemon

1 teaspoon vanilla extract

1. Preheat the oven to 350°F. Grease an 8-inch square baking pan with cooking spray. Arrange the berries in the pan.

2. In a blender, combine the eggs, sweetener, almond flour, cream, lemon zest and juice, and vanilla. Blend on low speed until well combined, about 1 minute. Pour the batter over the berries.

3. Bake for 40 minutes, or until the pudding is set and a toothpick inserted into the center comes out clean. Serve warm or chill in the refrigerator for at least 5 hours or until cold before serving.

ACTIVE TIME: 15 minutes

TOTAL TIME: 55 minutes

SERVINGS: 6

DIETARY CONSIDERATIONS

Vegetarian

MACROS

70% Fat

13% Carbs

13% Protein

PER SERVING

Calories: 150

Total Fat: 12g

Total Carbs: 16g

Net Carbs: 5g

Fiber: 3g

Sugar: 4g

Protein: 5g

PEANUT BUTTER-MAPLE MOUSSE

It's hard to believe something so simple can taste so good, but this little fat bomb shows you how easy it is to make a keto dessert that your non-keto kids can also enjoy. You can vary the nut butter to suit your preference, but don't omit the maple extract. It just makes this mousse.

4 ounces full-fat cream cheese, softened

3 tablespoons creamy no-sugar-added peanut butter

2 tablespoons Truvía granulated sweetener

½ cup half-and-half

¼ cup heavy cream

1 tablespoon maple extract

1. In the bowl of a stand mixer fitted with the paddle attachment, combine the cream cheese, peanut butter, sweetener, half-and-half, heavy cream, and maple extract. Beat on medium until creamy, fluffy, and well aerated, 3 to 4 minutes.

2. Divide among four small dessert dishes or ramekins. Cover and chill in the refrigerator until ready to serve.

ACTIVE TIME: 15 minutes

TOTAL TIME: 15 minutes

SERVINGS: 4

DIETARY CONSIDERATIONS

Egg-Free

Vegetarian

MACROS

80% Fat

7% Carbs

9% Protein

PER SERVING

Calories: 272

Total Fat: 24g

Total Carbs: 12g

Net Carbs: 5g

Fiber: 1g

Sugar: 4g

Protein: 6g

TWO-INGREDIENT CHEESECAKE MOUSSE

NO COOK

Yet another "barely a recipe" recipe, I first made this around the Fourth of July for a little festive fun. I put the mousse in individual cups, added blue coloring, topped them with whipped cream, and stuck in half a strawberry—and they were instantly gone. Something so simple to make and yet a hit? Definitely deserves its place in a cookbook.

ACTIVE TIME: 10 minutes

TOTAL TIME: 10 minutes (+1 hour chilling)

SERVINGS: 4

DIETARY CONSIDERATIONS

Egg-Free

Vegetarian

MACROS

91% Fat

5% Carbs

3% Protein

PER SERVING

Calories: 430

Total Fat: 43g

Total Carbs: 5g

Net Carbs: 5g

Fiber: 0g

Sugar: 4g

Protein: 3g

FOR THE MOUSSE

1 (1-ounce) box sugar-free instant cheesecake pudding mix, sifted

2 cups heavy cream

TO GARNISH (OPTIONAL)

4 teaspoons unsweetened flaked coconut, toasted

4 fresh strawberry slices

1. For the mousse: In a large bowl, combine the sifted pudding mix and cream. Beat with an electric mixer on medium until stiff peaks form.

2. Divide the mixture among four small dessert dishes or ramekins. Refrigerate until chilled, 1 to 2 hours.

3. If desired, top each mousse with 1 teaspoon coconut and a strawberry slice before serving.

OLD-FASHIONED CHOCOLATE PUDDING

Maybe I'm slow on the uptake, but it was not immediately obvious to me how to make a chocolate pudding with no flour, no cornstarch—no thickener at all, really. It kept me from trying things for a while, until one day I decided to just get in the kitchen and try something (anything!) so I could make some progress. I still can't believe my first attempt worked. But it did, which is good for all of us.

1 cup heavy cream

1 cup unsweetened almond milk

⅓ cup Truvía granulated sweetener

¼ cup unsweetened cocoa powder

1 large egg

1 teaspoon xanthan gum

1 teaspoon vanilla extract

Whipped cream, for serving

1. In a medium saucepan, combine the cream, almond milk, sweetener, cocoa powder, egg, and xanthan gum. Whisk until well combined. Cook over medium-low heat, whisking frequently, until the mixture coats the back of a spoon, about 6 to 8 minutes. (You may need to add a little extra xanthan gum to get to this point.) Do not let the mixture come to a rolling boil. You want to cook it gently and slowly.

2. Remove from the heat and whisk in the vanilla. Transfer to a serving bowl. Cover and chill in the refrigerator until the pudding has set, 2 to 4 hours.

3. Serve topped with whipped cream.

ACTIVE TIME: 20 minutes

TOTAL TIME: 20 minutes (+ 2 hours chilling)

SERVINGS: 4

DIETARY CONSIDERATIONS
Vegetarian

MACROS
88% Fat
6% Carbs
6% Protein

PER SERVING
Calories: 273
Total Fat: 27g
Total Carbs: 22g
Net Carbs: 4g
Fiber: 2g
Sugar: 2g
Protein: 5g

RASPBERRIES & CREAM

My mom used to make blancmange for us when we were sick. As a child I didn't really see the point of this simple, somewhat bland pudding. But as a grown-up, I can see how doctoring it up with a little lemon juice and a few berries can make a simple dessert just a little more sophisticated. It also looks very pretty, so it's good for company.

ACTIVE TIME: 20 minutes

TOTAL TIME: 35 minutes (+ 4 hours chilling)

SERVINGS: 8

DIETARY CONSIDERATIONS

Egg-Free

MACROS

82% Fat

7% Carbs

4% Protein

PER SERVING

Calories: 175

Total Fat: 16g

Total Carbs: 8g

Net Carbs: 3g

Fiber: 2g

Sugar: 3g

Protein: 2g

1 cup heavy cream

1 cup unsweetened almond milk

2 tablespoons Truvía granulated sweetener

¼ teaspoon unflavored powdered gelatin

1 cup full-fat sour cream

1 tablespoon lemon juice

1 tablespoon almond extract

1½ cups fresh or thawed frozen raspberries

1. In a medium saucepan, combine the cream, almond milk, and sweetener. Whisk until well combined. Slowly add the gelatin, whisking continuously. (You may see a few small lumps, but they will disappear when the mixture is heated.) Cook over medium heat, whisking frequently, until the gelatin and sweetener have completely dissolved.

2. Place the saucepan in the refrigerator to cool for 15 to 20 minutes. Whisk in the sour cream, lemon juice, and almond extract until the mixture is smooth.

3. Crush the raspberries with the back of a spoon to create a rough puree. Divide the crushed raspberries among eight 4-ounce ramekins. Pour the cream mixture over the top of the berries.

4. Cover and refrigerate for at least 4 hours or up to 24 hours before serving.

VEGAN NO-COOK CHOCOLATE PUDDING

Nope, it doesn't taste like tofu, I promise you! I know some of you who are keto stay away from soy, and if that's you, then be sure to enjoy the Old-Fashioned Chocolate Pudding on page 230. But it's hard to beat this one for simplicity and taste—not to mention the evil joy of making your unsuspecting family eat tofu and like it.

16 ounces soft silken tofu

¾ cup Truvía granulated sweetener, plus more if needed

¼ cup unsweetened cocoa powder, plus more if needed

½ teaspoon ground cinnamon, plus more if needed

¼ cup unsweetened almond milk, if needed

1. In a blender, combine the tofu, sweetener, cocoa powder, and cinnamon. Blend on high speed until the mixture is smooth. (If it's too thick for your blender, add a little almond milk. Use as little liquid as necessary, as you want the pudding to set up during chilling.) Taste the pudding and add additional sweetener, cocoa powder, or cinnamon, if desired.

2. Divide among four small dessert dishes or ramekins. Cover and chill in the refrigerator until set, 6 to 8 hours.

ACTIVE TIME: 10 minutes

TOTAL TIME: 10 minutes (+ 6 hours chilling)

SERVINGS: 4

DIETARY CONSIDERATIONS

Egg-Free

Dairy-Free

Vegan

MACROS

47% Fat

21% Carbs

32% Protein

PER SERVING

Calories: 78

Total Fat: 4g

Total Carbs: 42g

Net Carbs: 4g

Fiber: 2g

Sugar: 0g

Protein: 6g

VEGAN PIE CRUST

We ate a lot of pie crust at my house the week I was trying to get a good pie crust recipe down. I wanted something fuss-free—because if you're making a pie crust, you're making a filling. Spending a lot of time on filling *and* crust is about the point where I just decide I don't really need a crust. But with this easy pie crust, I don't really have an excuse not to make it.

1 cup superfine blanched almond flour

2 tablespoons Swerve confectioners' sweetener

¼ cup coconut oil, melted

1. Preheat the oven to 400°F.

2. In a medium bowl, combine the almond flour and sweetener. Whisk until well combined. Add the melted coconut oil and stir until the mixture has a crumbly texture.

3. Transfer the mixture to a shallow 9-inch pie pan. Pat it evenly into the bottom and up the sides of the pan.

4. Bake for 8 to 10 minutes. If the edges begin to brown faster than the rest of the crust, cover the edges with foil or reduce the oven temperature to 375°F.

5. Cool the crust on a wire rack for at least 30 minutes before filling.

RECIPE NOTE

French Silk Pudding (page 212) is a perfect filling for this crust.

ACTIVE TIME: 10 minutes

TOTAL TIME: 18 minutes (+ 30 minutes cooling)

SERVINGS: 8

DIETARY CONSIDERATIONS

Egg-Free

Dairy-Free

Vegan

MACROS

87% Fat

3% Carbs

9% Protein

PER SERVING

Calories: 141

Total Fat: 14g

Total Carbs: 5g

Net Carbs: 1g

Fiber: 2g

Sugar: 1g

Protein: 3g

KETO SHAKES & SMOOTHIES

This chart is meant for you to mix and match to your heart's content. While you should definitely experiment to figure out which flavors you want more or less of, I want to give you some general guidelines to get started. The most important thing to remember is this: Would you consider drinking a cup of cream, eating 1 cup of berries, and washing it all down with ¼ cup of peanut butter all in one go? No? Then don't put that much stuff into your smoothie either. It's very easy to overdo the calories in a shake.

As a general rule, I suggest picking an item from each column: liquid, protein, fat, and extras. Depending on what you pick, start with:

1	cup liquid (if you're using ice, use ¾ cup liquid and ¼ cup ice)
¼	cup soft protein such as tofu, full-fat Greek yogurt, or full-fat cottage cheese, OR 1 scoop protein powder
1	tablespoon fat such as no-sugar-added peanut butter, almond butter, etc.
¼	cup berries
1	tablespoon flavorings such as unsweetened cocoa powder, flaxseeds, or chia seeds
½ to 1	teaspoon spices such as ground cinnamon, pumpkin pie spice, etc. (but ¼ teaspoon ground nutmeg since that tends to be a fairly strong flavor)

NAME	LIQUID	PROTEIN	FAT	EXTRAS
ALMOND HORCHATA	almond milk	vanilla protein powder	almond butter	ground cinnamon
STRAWBERRY-BANANA SMOOTHIE	almond milk	banana protein powder	coconut oil	¼ cup strawberries
CHOCOLATE PEANUT BUTTER	high-protein milk	½ cup soft tofu	peanut butter	1 Tbsp unsweetened dark cocoa powder
MINT LASSI	water	full-fat Greek yogurt	butter	fresh or dried mint
CARDAMOM SMOOTHIE	hemp milk	full-fat cottage cheese	almond butter	ground cardamom
GREEN SMOOTHIE	almond milk	vanilla protein powder	coconut oil	2 cups spinach
PEPPERMINT SHAKE	almond milk	chocolate protein powder	butter	peppermint extract
PUMPKIN PIE SHAKE	water	full-fat Greek yogurt + pure pumpkin puree	almond butter	pumpkin pie spice
RASPBERRY SHAKE	milk	unflavored protein powder	walnuts	½ cup raspberries
AVOCADO SMOOTHIE	almond milk	vanilla protein powder	avocado	ground nutmeg
COFFEE SHAKE	strong coffee	full-fat Greek yogurt	coconut oil	ground cinnamon
CASHEW CREAM SHAKE	hemp milk	vanilla protein powder	¼ cup cashews	ground cardamom
CINNAMON ROLL SHAKE	almond milk	vanilla protein powder	full-fat Greek yogurt	ground cinnamon
MINT GREEN SMOOTHIE	coconut milk	vanilla protein powder or mint cookie protein powder	avocado	mint extract
CHOCOLATE-ALMOND SHAKE	coconut milk	chocolate protein powder	almonds	chia or flaxseeds

STRAWBERRY-BANANA
SMOOTHIE

PUMPKIN PIE SHAKE

RASPBERRY SHAKE

GREEN SMOOTHIE

ALMOND HORCHATA

KETO SALAD DRESSINGS

Commercial dressings are often full of corn oil, sugar, and thickeners that many of us try to avoid while on keto. But once you see how easy it is to make dressings at home, and how much tastier they are, you may never again waste your time at the grocery store, standing around reading labels, hoping to find a keto-friendly salad dressing.

NAME	ACID	FAT	HERBS	
ASIAN DRESSING	¼ cup rice vinegar 1 Tbsp soy sauce	¼ cup extra-virgin olive oil ¼ cup sesame oil		
ASIAN PEANUT DRESSING*	2 Tbsp rice vinegar 2 Tbsp soy sauce juice of 1 lime	¼ cup no-sugar-added peanut butter		
BALSAMIC VINAIGRETTE	¼ cup balsamic vinegar	½ cup extra-virgin olive oil		
BLUE CHEESE DRESSING	¼ cup red wine vinegar	½ cup full-fat sour cream or mayonnaise	1 tsp dried chives ½ tsp garlic powder ½ tsp onion powder	
COLESLAW DRESSING	¼ cup apple cider vinegar 1 Tbsp lemon juice	½ cup full-fat sour cream or mayonnaise		
CILANTRO-JALAPEÑO DRESSING*		½ cup full-fat sour cream	½ cup chopped fresh cilantro	
CREAMY CURRIED DRESSING	1 Tbsp lemon juice	½ cup full-fat Greek yogurt	1 tsp curry powder	

*Blend ingredients together

SPICES	AROMATICS	SWEETENERS	ADDITIONAL INGREDIENTS
	1 tsp grated fresh ginger		toasted sesame seeds
salt, pepper	1 tsp minced fresh ginger 1 tsp minced garlic		¼ cup hot water
salt, pepper			
salt, pepper			1 tsp Worcestershire sauce ¼ cup crumbled blue cheese
salt, pepper		1 packet Splenda	
½ jalapeño salt	6 garlic cloves		
salt, cayenne pepper			

continued...

ASIAN DRESSING

CREAMY CURRIED
DRESSING

BALSAMIC VINAIGRETTE

ITALIAN DRESSING

RANCH DRESSING

NAME	ACID	FAT	HERBS	
FRENCH DRESSING	¼ cup red wine vinegar	½ cup extra-virgin olive oil		
GINGER DRESSING	¼ cup rice vinegar 1 Tbsp soy sauce	½ cup peanut oil	¼ cup chopped scallions	
GREEK DRESSING	¼ cup red wine vinegar	½ cup extra-virgin olive oil	1 tsp dried oregano ½ tsp dried rosemary ½ tsp dried dill	
ITALIAN DRESSING	¼ cup red wine vinegar	½ cup extra-virgin olive oil	parsley oregano fresh basil	
MUSTARD DRESSING*	¼ cup apple cider vinegar 1 tsp soy sauce	½ cup extra-virgin olive oil		
RANCH DRESSING	¼ cup red wine vinegar	½ cup full-fat sour cream or mayonnaise	1 tsp dried chives ½ tsp garlic powder ½ tsp onion powder	
TAHINI DRESSING*	¼ cup apple cider vinegar 1 tsp lemon juice	½ cup tahini		
THYME DIP	2 tsp lemon juice	½ cup mayonnaise	2 Tbsp minced fresh thyme	

*Blend ingredients together

SPICES	AROMATICS	SWEETENERS	ADDITIONAL INGREDIENTS
pinch of paprika		1 packet Splenda	2 tsp ketchup 1 tsp Worcestershire sauce
	1 Tbsp minced fresh ginger	1 packet Splenda	
salt, pepper	4 garlic cloves, minced		
salt, pepper	4 garlic cloves, minced		
salt, pepper	2 garlic cloves, minced	1 packet Splenda	1 Tbsp Dijon mustard
salt, pepper			1 tsp Worcestershire sauce
salt, pepper	4 garlic cloves, minced		2 Tbsp hot water
salt, pepper	2 Tbsp minced red onion		

INDEX

NOTE: Page references in *italics* refer to photos of recipes.

COCONUT FUDGE
page 142

COCONUT FUDGE
page 142